NODOROC

and

THE BOHURONS

With excerpts from
The Early History of Jackson County Georgia
by
G.J.N. Wilson

Richard L. Thornton
and
Marilyn A. Rae

ANCIENT CYPRESS PRESS
Fort Lauderdale

Ancient Cypress Press
Fort Lauderdale
Florida, USA
www.ancientcypresspress.com

ISBN: 978-0-9889648-7-7

Cover illustration by Mary Rae

CONTENTS

INTRODUCTION

La Entrada al Infierno
The Gateway to Hell

NODOROC

Virtual reality image by Richard Thornton, Architect

" I am utterly unable to describe the scene or to express in words the feelings
it produces. When I take into consideration the associations connected with
it and with the other more awful one described in the word of God I am so
overcome with the comparison suggested that I can think only of St. John's
words in Revelation—'And the smoke of their torment ascendeth up for
ever and ever.' "

The Gateway to Hell

Grim, gray, acrid smoke rises from an island of stunted, singed trees on a sea of grasses, shrubs and free-standing nut trees. The smells of charred or rotting flesh permeate the air, when the wind blows the right direction. In the shadows, a giant, black, four legged creature with massive claws, a forked tongue and a long tail, constantly wagging, crunches and smacks on the decaying carcass of an herbivore, who strayed into the quicksand and couldn't get out.

The reader immediately imagines this scene to be somewhere in the embryonic plains of western North America or central Africa . . . perhaps 50 to 80 million years ago. It is not. This macabre image of the past was reality only blink of God's eye away, a little over 200 years ago. The place is now adjacent to a county airport in the northeastern sector of the Atlanta, Georgia Metropolitan Area. How could this be . . . a volcano in the flower-scented, forest landscape of the Peach State?

Human Sacrifice at a Stone Temple

A bound, sacrificial victim is led by a group of priests and armed men along a path through hideous gnarled trees. The path leads to a triangular, stone temple, built in the profile of a pyramid. As the party arrives before the temple, the chief priest steps out of its portal, his face distorted by fumes of a gas that seeps from the earth. He beckons the soldiers, holding the living sacrifice in the small temple. Paralyzed by fear, the sacrificial victim is placed on a stone altar within.

The young person' throat is quickly slashed by a dagger. His or her blood drains down a channel into a sacred bowl. The blood is drunk by the priests and political leaders, then, at the end of the ceremony, the pale body of the sacrifice is tossed into a red hot pool, whose blue flames quickly turn the once-living flesh into charcoal.

The reader is quickly taken back to memories of an Indiana Jones movie, or perhaps, if he or she is more knowledgeable of ancient history, knows that we have described a human sacrifice on the islands of Crete or Cyprus, three to four millenniums ago. They are wrong. The place again is the location near a county airport in metropolitan Atlanta.

How could this be? Until recently, everyone knew that the indigenous peoples of Georgia never built out of stone. The existence of a previously ignored, advanced Native culture was forced down the throats of protesting archaeologists in 2012, but even then, everyone acknowledged that these structures contained walls of stacked field stones, not rectangular blocks from a quarry. Relatively few structures in Mexico even contain quarried stones. In the Americas, they are almost entirely confined to the Andean civilizations of South America.

The temple was destroyed in the early 1800s, but fortunately measured before becoming the fireplaces and lawn furniture of a wealthy planter. Some of the stones sit in a museum. The temple built out of quarried stones really existed.

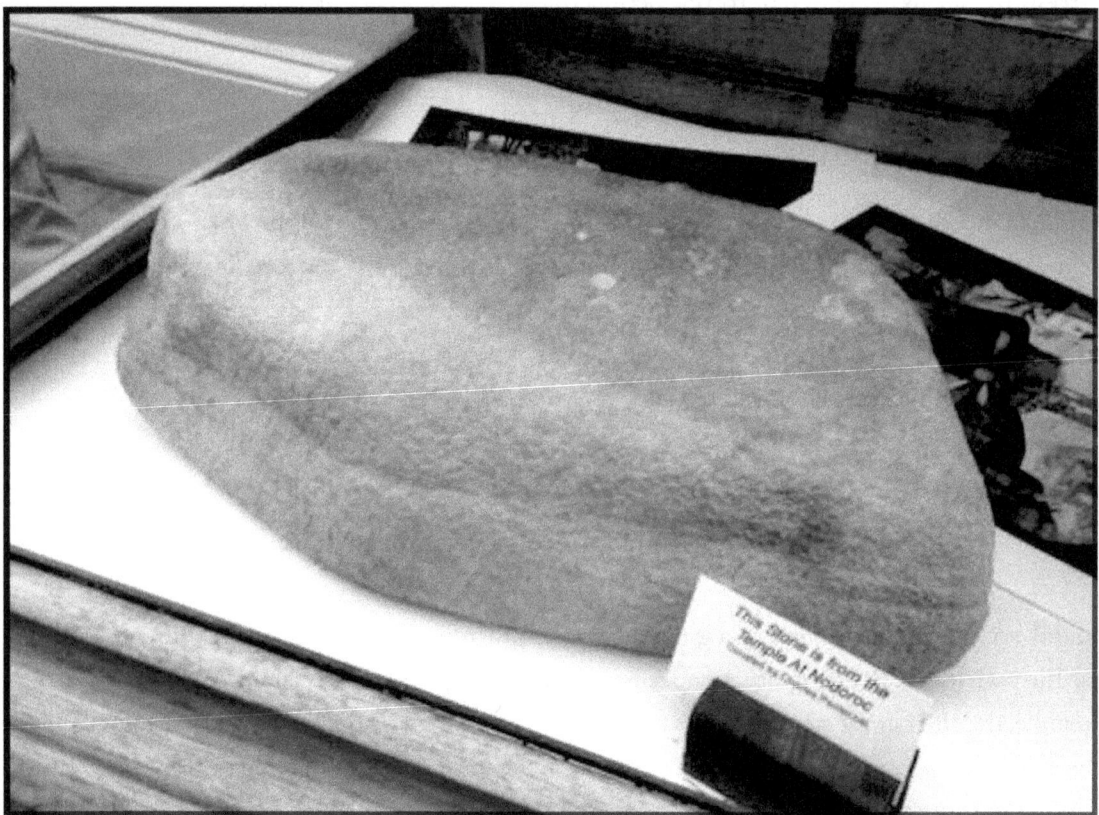

Stone from the Temple at Nodoroc

Courtesy of Winder-Barrow County Historical Museum

By the time that the Creek Indians occupied what is now called the State of Georgia, human sacrifice ceased, because the Creeks were mono-theists who did not believe in human sacrifice. However, they knew of this evil place of noxious fumes, lethal heat and blue flames. They called it the "Gateway to Hell." It was still a place of death, however. It was reserved for the execution of captured enemies, who had committed atrocities against civilians and for their fellow countrymen, who had committed the most heinous of crimes.

Riders in the Storm

A band of men ride their horses across the landscape. They have tan skin and wear brightly colored clothing. Their names are Arabic, Hebrew, Spanish and French in origin. They are known as fierce warriors who raid the rural farmsteads of peasants without warning. We are obviously describing a band of mercenaries in Iberia or France during the middle and late feudal periods. During the 700s vast Muslim armies quickly overran most of Iberia and the Gothic kingdom in southern France. Several Muslim armies temporarily penetrated into central France, but by the 800s the Muslim-Christian frontier was roughly the Pyrenees. For 780 years afterward, Christian armies from Gothlandia (Languedoc and Catalon), Galicia, Gallia (France), Navarre, Gasconia, Bascia (Euskal Herria), Asturia, Portugal, then ultimately, Castille and Aragon, intermittently fought their way southward until 1491, when no lands in Iberia were ruled by Muslims. This series of wars are labeled *La Reconquista* in Spain and Portugal.

During the *Reconquista*, numerous independent bands of professional soldiers formed in medieval France and Iberia. They would often switch sides according to who paid them the most. Perhaps the most famous Christian warrior of Iberia, Rodrigo Díaz de Vivar, is better known by his Arabic name, *Al Cid* (The Lord.) Rodrigo's first battle experience was as a mercenary for a Moorish king against the army of a Christian king. He then led Christian armies against the Umayyad Muslims in Andalusia, then commanded a band of Christian and Muslim mercenaries against a massive invasion of North African Muslim fundamentalists, and finally, for the remainder of his life, ruled a powerful kingdom in which Christian and Muslim Iberians lived in harmony.

Mercenaries were initially called *barónes* in Christian lands and *Hasham Al-Nasara Khayl* in Moorish Andalusia. The Christian mercenaries were later called *routier* in Western Europe, while a man of lower nobility, who either hired or led them, became known as a *baron* in France, a *hidalgo* in Castille and Aragon, or a *fidalgo* in Galicia, Navarre and Portugal. Much of the Christian recovery of Iberia was accomplished by hidalgos, who raised their own private armies, captured a chunk of Muslim territory then ruled that territory as a vassal of a Christian king. The same system was used in the creation of the vast Spanish empire in the Americas.

There is one problem with this historic interpretation when applied to our scenario of the galloping, polyglot, horsemen. The location was northeastern Georgia and the time was the middle 1700s, when Georgia was supposedly a royal colony of Great Britain. How could this be?

Northern Georgia's Hidden History

Sir Winston Churchill stated, "*The winners get to write the history books*." No better example of this axiom can be found than in the official histories of the Southeastern section of the United States. By 1763, Great Britain had won all the marbles from France. By 1721, the United States had won all the remaining marbles from Spain. A version of history was taught to subsequent generations that erased the advanced indigenous populations, barely mentioned early French exploration and marginalized Spain's colonial activities. The bulk of the population in the eastern United States believed that brave Anglo-Saxon and Scottish pioneers had hacked a civilization out of the virginal wilderness.

Beginning in the early 1900s and accelerating during the federally funded archaeological studies at Depression Era WPA projects, plus reservoirs built by the Tennessee Valley Authority and Corps of Engineers in the latter half of the 20th century, anthropologists began piecing together an understanding of the Southeast's pre-European past. At the tail end of the 20th century, foundation and university-funded archaeological studies began resurrecting the history of Spanish missions in the Southeast. The role of early French explorers and colonists in the Southeast remain obscured. The true colonial history of the Southern Appalachians remains a taboo subject that most archaeologists are loath to discuss. They do not want to step on political toes.

One of several texts, which provide glimpses into the true history of the Colonial Period in the lower Southeastern United States is, "*The Early History of Jackson County, Georgia,*" by Gustavus James Nash Wilson. Jackson was one of the earliest counties created in northeastern Georgia after the American Revolution. From it was spawned Clarke and Barrow Counties in the early 1800s. All three counties are now very affluent, populated and part of the Atlanta Megapolis.

Gustavus James Nash Wilson was born in Jackson County in 1826, after it was no longer on the frontier. In fact, by that time it was becoming one of the most affluent and progressive counties in Georgia. However, Wilson's father had been one of Jackson County's first Anglo-American settlers. Throughout much of the 1800s, the Wilsons had Creek Indian neighbors, who had somehow avoided deportation to Alabama, and then Oklahoma. There were quite a few legitimate Creek families in rural northeast Georgia until the mid-1900s, when first the Depression and then, World War II, scattered families to the wind. In that context, Wilson's history may be considered a credible, almost eyewitness account, of the frontier in the Georgia Piedmont.

Crawford W. Long, a brilliant surgeon, moved to the town of Jefferson in Jackson County, during 1842, because it was considered a boom town, destined to grow. He became the first doctor in the world to use sulfuric ether as anesthesia in Jefferson. In a few years, the construction of a railroad terminus in Fulton County, to the southwest, would cause its county seat, Atlanta, to boom into the regional center that Jefferson dreamed of becoming.

Gustavus Wilson was essentially a self-educated man. His formal education was limited to a few years of attendance at a field school near his home as a child. However, he devoured any books that he could borrow off of neighbors. By age 13, his knowledge was so admired that he was asked to be the TEACHER of a new primary school in nearby Commerce, GA. He was a professional teacher for thirteen years until enlisting in Company E, 34th Georgia Infantry Regiment of the CSA's Army of Tennessee. He miraculously survived the Civil War and surrendered with General Johnston near Durham, North Carolina on April 17, 1865. After the Civil War, Wilson became a carpenter and builder. He was elected Commissioner of the Jackson County Board of Education in 1871 and held that position for over 30 years. By 1871, he was considered to own one of the finest private libraries in northeastern Georgia.

Wilson himself did not publish the book. He had been dead about five years, when the book was printed in 1914. William Ellis White, a printer in Jefferson, GA, assembled and edited the manuscripts, memoirs and newspaper articles of Wilson into a book format. However, the book contains an affidavit in the front produced by the Jackson County Board of Education in 1913 that affirms Wilson's history. Wilson was a former Chairman of the Board of Education. White stated that he traveled to multiple locations in several states to confirm the accuracy of Wilson's manuscript.

While always a popular book with local historians, the contents of Wilson's book did not make it into the official state history texts in Georgia. Those few academicians who were aware of the book, dismissed its accounts of 18th century Georgia as being frontier folklore. Wilson's stories did not seem to fit into the orthodoxy of Anglo-American history.

In reality, though, it is Wilson's straightforward, almost naïve description, and discussion of Nodoroc, the Wog and the Bohurons that give him credibility. The words and events seemed improbable to academicians of the 20th century. However, Wilson was not trying to prove any particular theory about history. He was merely leaving a legacy about a way of life that was gone with the wind.

The chapters in Wilson's book that describe the Native Americans and frontier era should not be considered an absolutely reliable authority on all things. The Creek words he heard as a youth were often altered in his memory forty years later, when he wrote the manuscript. He also obviously embellished or even fictionalized sections of his stories about the Native Americans with inaccurate cultural details, such as calling their log houses, wigwams. Many or most of the conversations between persons, whom he never knew, are certainly fabricated. However, overall, "*The Early History of Jackson County*" is invaluable resource for understanding the Northeast Georgia's forgotten past.

The Counties Created from the Original Jackson County

Although a rural county when the book was published, Jackson County is now on the northern edge of both the Atlanta and Athens Metropolitan Statistical Areas. Its county seat is Jefferson. It is located in northeastern quadrant of Georgia, along the Interstate 85 corridor. Although not officially in a metropolitan area, Jackson is currently much more suburban in "feeling" than agricultural.

Clarke County is located immediately southeast of contemporary Jackson County. Its county seat is Athens. Clarke was broken off from Jackson County in the early 1800s. Because of the enormous economic impact of the University of Georgia during the late 20th Century, the population of Clarke County has swollen to give the Athens, Clarke County, Madison County, Oconee County and Oglethorpe County area metropolitan status.

Barrow County is located southwest of contemporary Jackson County. Its county seat is Winder. Barrow was also broken off from the original boundaries of Jackson County in the early 1800s. Barrow is a booming county that is part of the Atlanta Metropolitan Statistical Area. Both the Interstate 85 Corridor and the U. S. 78 Corridor between Atlanta and Athens. The Nodoroc is located near the Winder-Barrow County Airport.

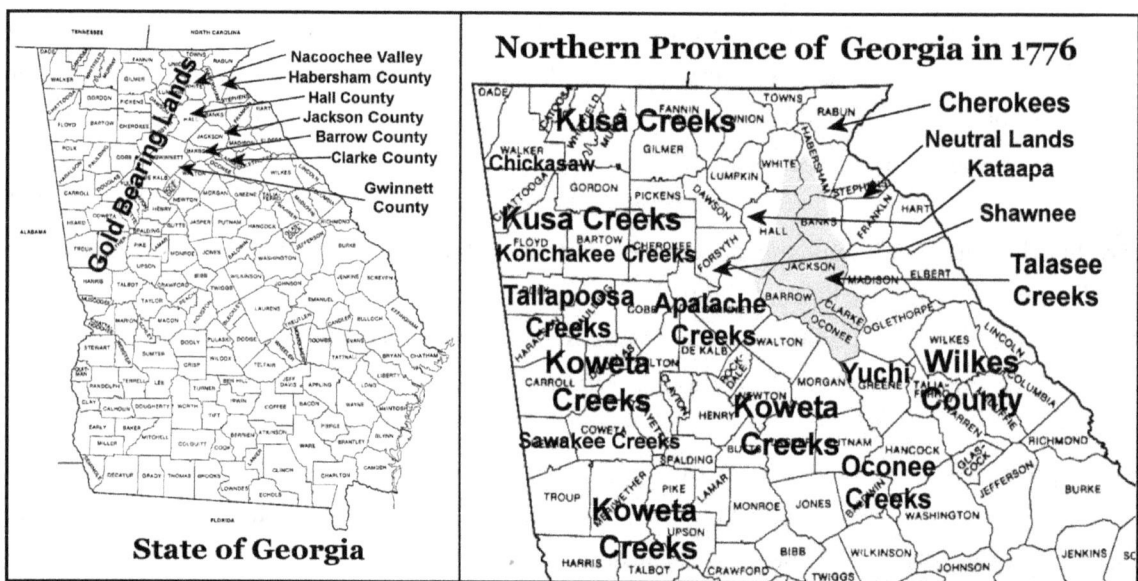

Map by Richard Thornton, Architect

CHAPTER ONE

La Tierra Desconocida
The Unknown Land

Creek Dancers

Courtesy of Perdido Bay Muscogee-Creek Tribe

The Unknown Land

Very little that Georgia's students are told about the Colonial Era history in the northern part of the state is accurate. What they learn is a handful of frontier misinterpretations and folk stories that have little to do with the region's actual history. Only two of Georgia's state historical markers having to do with Native American occupation of the region are accurate. They are the markers for Etowah Mounds near Cartersville and New Echota, the last Cherokee capital, near Calhoun.

One of the principal causes of this disinformation is that British maps left most of northern Georgia blank after 1693. French maps continued to show the changes in the ethnic groups of the Southern Highlands until 1763, when it lost its North American possessions. Until then, France claimed all of the region drained by the Ohio, Tennessee, Alabama-Coosa and Mississippi River systems.

During the 1680s and 1690s, French engineers and traders mapped all of the major rivers in the Southeast, west of the Blue Ridge Mountains. The maps showed specific locations of ethnic groups and major towns. The French explorers were not able to paddle up the French Broad River because of dangerous rapids near Hot Springs, NC. The area around Asheville was left blank, but 18th century British colonial records place a large Shawnee town at Asheville's location until 1763.

There would be no map that accurately portrayed the locations of northern Georgia's rivers until 1838. The mountain ridges would not be accurately mapped until acquired by the U. S. Forest Service in the mid-20th century. The contents of the Colonial Era maps will be discussed in Chapter Two.

Georgia's Native Americans in the 1700s

All of the histories of North Georgia that proliferate on the internet these days tend to have the same story. They state that in pre-European times the Cherokees and the "mound builders" shared northern Georgia.

Some go on to explain that the "mound builders" were *probably* the ancestors of the Creek Indians. Most of the articles then state that all of northern Georgia was occupied by the Cherokee Indians, when English settlers arrived in the Southeast.

The facts are further confused by historians and anthropologists, who use terms like *Overhill Cherokees* or *Muskogee Creeks* for the period before 1725 when neither tribe existed. Academicians tend to replicate each others' "facts" rather than go to the primary resource. They don't look at the maps for specific periods in history and tend to frame events in the nomenclature of 21st century federally recognized tribes.

The true history of the Southern Highlands and Piedmont is quite different. Several indigenous ethnic groups inhabited the region when Europeans first arrived in the Southeast. In the valleys, population density was very high. Beginning around 1500, European diseases began to spread inland from the Gulf of Mexico and Atlantic Coast. The scale of the pathogenic onslaught was magnified by the Spanish expeditions into the interior during the mid and late 1500s. Demographers have estimated that the population dropped in the Southeast as much as 90% during the 1500s and early 1600s due to European pathogens.

None of these people were called the Cherokee or Creek Indians until well into the 18th century. The first mention of the "Charakees" on a map was in 1717. The first label of "Creek Indians" did not appear on a European map until Emmanuel Bowens' map of Georgia was published in 1747. However, all of the major provinces of the Creek Confederacy were mentioned by the chroniclers of the Hernando de Soto Expedition, which passed through Georgia, the Carolinas, Tennessee and Alabama in 1540. Those same chronicles did not mention the Cherokee Indians or any people speaking the Cherokee language.

In 1700 the Blue Ridge Mountains and upper Piedmont in the future state of Georgia were dominated by the Apalache, a proto-Creek people, who had once controlled a multi-ethnic confederacy that spanned from southwestern Virginia to southern Georgia. Northwestern Georgia was occupied by the Kusa, later known as Upper Creeks, and the Conchakee, a people related to the Mountain Apalache, who also occupied the lower Chattahoochee River. The extreme northwestern corner of Georgia was occupied by branches of the Chickasaws, known as the Ustanauli, Napoche and Chikamauga. Shawnee and Yuchi villages were located along the Savannah River. The Shawnee gave their local name (Savano) to the Savannah River. At that time, there was a concentration of Europeans and mestizos in the vicinity of the Nacoochee Valley in northeast Georgia.

British colonial authorities created the Cherokee Indian tribe. Initially, authorities in Charleston encouraged a cluster of eight villages with Itsate Creek names on the headwaters of the Savannah River to jointly negotiate with them. At that time, they were labeled Chora-te (Itsate Creek) or Chora-ke (Muskogee Creek). These are words that mean "splinter people." The 1717 map published by French cartographer, Guilluam DeLisle, labeled the cluster of villages on the Savannah River headwaters and a larger cluster on the Holston and French Broad River in northeast Tennessee, the Charaqui.

In 1725, Colonel George Chicken of South Carolina met with 14 bands of people in the Southern Appalachians and encouraged them to create a formal tribe with a king. This is the beginning of the Cherokee Tribe. A map of South Carolina produced that year showed five villages in the extreme northeast corner of the future state of Georgia being in that new Cherokee Tribe.

By 1732, only one Cherokee village was shown on the maps to be in the future state of Georgia. It was Tugaloo, and it was on an island in the river that would eventually be the boundary between South Carolina and Georgia. Apparently, the villages had been abandoned because of the 40 year long Creek-Cherokee War. Cherokee villages again appeared in extreme northeastern Georgia after 1763. Between 1763 and the mid-1780s, the total Cherokee population in northern Georgia was probably in the range of 200-300 people.

At least by 1760, all Native American peoples in northern Georgia were living in log houses and using muskets almost exclusively for hunting and warfare. The change to firearms began in the mid-1600s and was complete by 1720. By the 1760s, North Georgia's Natives were raising livestock and living on farmsteads, not significantly different from those of European settlers.

Gustavus Wilson, or the editor of his manuscript, inserted several Native American words and customs into "The Early History of Jackson." The Creek winter house is called a *choko*, from the Itza Maya word for warm. The Creek summer house, a light structure woven from split cane, saplings and vines, is called a *chiki*, from the Itza Maya word for house. The words *wigwam* and *wickiup* were never used in the Southeastern United States.

Historical Markers

Twenty-first century historical markers and official state histories provide a very different version of history than is found on the Colonial Period maps. They often contradict each other. Even though much more accurate information is available, the version of history that these markers present is what Georgia students typically read.

Cherokee Town of Quanasee – Hayesville, NC

Hayesville is located in the Clay County, NC, immediately north of Brasstown Bald Mountain, GA. It was not a real town. By the mid 1720s it contained a little over 100 residents. Contemporary descriptions of the village site, such as by William Bartram, make no mention of a mound. The pre-European town with mounds may have been some distance away from the Colonial Period Cherokee village.

A historical marker has been installed in the Quanassee Archaeological Zone. The sign claims that the mound was built by the Cherokees. However, the sign also provides some other information directly related to Georgia Colonial Era history. It says that the village was burned several times, beginning in 1725, by Upper Creeks living nearby in Georgia. Eventually, the village was abandoned after being burned in 1754, because of being so close to Creek territory in the Georgia Mountains.

What is particularly interesting about this sign is that in a North Carolina county a sign says that the Cherokees were on the losing end of the Creek-Cherokee War, and that traditional Creek territory was only a few miles away in Georgia. Another sign, erected by the Eastern Band of Cherokees at the Spikebuck Mound states that the Creek-Cherokee War ended in 1752, when actually it continued until 1754.

Battle of Taliwa – Ball Ground, GA

Visitors to Ball Ground, GA near the Etowah River in Cherokee County are greeted with two state historical markers on the main drag. The first one they see welcomes them to the site of the Cherokee town of Ball Ground. A nearby Mississippian Period mound marks the supposed center of that town. The sign goes on to state that in an Indian stickball game played at Ball Ground, the Cherokees defeated the Creeks and won all of northern Georgia.

No 18th or 19th century map shows a Cherokee village named Ball Ground on the Etowah River. Even maps of the Old Cherokee Nation by the Museum of the Cherokee Indian and the New Echota State Museum do not mention such a village.

Visitors to Ball Ground may drive a little farther on the main drag and read another state historical marker. This sign tells the reader that the famous Battle of Taliwa was fought in 1755, near a Creek Indian town named Taliwa, which was located where Ball Ground now is situated. In this battle the Cherokees only had 800 warriors, but were attacking a Creek town with 2000 warriors. The sign does not say that the Cherokees had traveled about 100 miles from the Little Tennessee River Valley near Loudon, TN to attack this Creek town.

What the sign does say is that the outnumbered Cherokees made four unsuccessful assaults. Then

Nanyehi, the 16 year old wife of a slain warrior, picked up a musket and began firing. She then led the fifth and successful assault on the village. By winning the battle, the Cherokees won all of northern Georgia. Nanyehi remarried an English trader named Brian Ward, and then became a great friend of the white man. She changed her name to Nancy Ward.

The Colony of Georgia kept detailed records on the Creek Confederacy because the Creeks and Georgians were close allies. There is no record of any Creek town named Taliwa. Taliwa is the word for "town" among the branch of the Creeks that lived in the Florida Panhandle and southeast tip of Alabama. The Itsate Creeks in the Georgia Mountains used the word "tula" for a major town. At any rate there were no Creek towns with 2,000 warriors in the 1700s, or even anything approaching 2,000 residents.

In 2008, a team of history and law professors from the University of Oklahoma spent two weeks examining the colonial archives of South Carolina and Georgia. They found no mention of a Battle of Taliwa or of the Cherokee Indians occupying all of northern Georgia. What they did find were numerous letters exchanged between South Carolina and Georgia in 1754 and 1755 concerning the catastrophic losses that the Cherokees were suffering in battles with the Koweta Creeks and Upper Creeks. It was feared that the Cherokees would not be able to honor their commitment to assist the British Crown in its war with France, or might even cease to exist.

The Colony of Georgia pressured and bribed the Creek town of Koweta to stop its attacks on the Cherokees. By the time that Koweta agreed to sign a peace treaty in late 1754, it had defeated the entire Cherokee Nation and recaptured all territories in Georgia and North Carolina that the Cherokees had conquered since 1714. In the process, 32 Cherokee chiefs had been executed.

In 1755 Upper Creeks, allied with France, gained back all their territories lost since 1725. They and the Cherokees made a peace treaty in which the Cherokees agreed to cease furnishing warriors to the British. So in 1755, the Cherokees and Georgia Creeks were at peace. Meanwhile, the Tennessee Overhill Cherokees, who supposedly captured Taliwa, were being badly whipped by France's Indian allies 153 miles away from Ball Ground in the Little Tennessee River Valley.

Battle of Blood Mountain – Union County, GA

At Neels Gap on US Highway 19-129 between Dahlonega and Blairsville, GA, is another state historic marker relating to the 40 year long Creek-Cherokee War (1715-1755). It states that the long war between the Creeks and Cherokees came to a dramatic end in a massive battle on the slopes of Blood Mountain at Slaughter Gap. The Cherokees won all of northern Georgia because of their victory at this battlefield.

As further proof of the battle, the sign states that early white settlers observed many human skeletons around Slaughter Gap along with thousands of arrowheads . . . hence the origin of the names Blood Mountain and Slaughter Gap.

As stated earlier, the Cherokees suffered catastrophic defeats at the hands of the Koweta and Upper Creeks at the end of the Creek-Cherokee War. From the first time that the Cherokees entered the history books in 1717, they fought with weapons of European manufacture . . . muskets, tomahawks and knives. In 1730 a delegation of famous Cherokee leaders and warriors visited London. They were challenged to an archery contest by some Englishmen and lost badly because they were so unaccustomed to shooting bows.

The Creeks were using muskets as early as the Battle of the Flint River in 1703, when they nearly wiped out an invading Spanish Army. There is another hole in this story told by this historical marker. The descendants of the Coosa (Upper) Creeks, who made life miserable for the Cherokees at Quanasee, continue to live along Coosa Creek in Union and Fannin Counties to this day. That is why Coosa Creek is called Coosa Creek. There might have been a battle fought at Slaughter Gap at some time in the past, but it was not between the Creeks and Cherokees.

Nacoochee Mound – White County, GA

The state historical marker states that Cherokees built this mound in the Nacoochee Valley. It also states that the Cherokee village around the mound was named Guaxule and that it was visited by Hernando de Soto in 1540.

The Nacoochee Mound was excavated in 1916 by professional archaeologists and found to contain artifacts associated with the proto-Creek cultures of central Georgia. The village around it was excavated by archaeologists from the university of Georgia in the early 2000s. Only artifacts associated with pre-European Muskogeans and Historic Period Creeks were found on the village site.

There is no evidence that Hernando de Soto passed through the Georgia Mountains. The word, Guaxule is the Castilian spelling of the Creek word for southerners. It has no meaning in Cherokee. A map drawn in 1693 by English cartographer, Robert Morden, showed the Creek town of Apalache being located in the Nacoochee Valley. A map drawn of the valley in the early 1700s showed the Creek towns of Nokose (Bear) and Itsate (Itza Maya People.) being located there. The Cherokee word "Noguchee" is a mispronunciation of Nokose.

Tugaloo Mounds – Stephens County, GA

The state historical marker, erected around 1970, states that Cherokees built the mounds and town of Tugaloo on an island in the Tugaloo River around 1450 AD. "Here, Cherokee priests maintained a sacred fire in the temple on top of the largest mound." The contents of the state historic marker are repeated in dozens of local histories, tourist brochures and even in Wikipedia.

The Tugaloo Archaeological Site was excavated by a team of archaeologists from the University of Georgia between 1957 and 1958. The project director, Dr. Joseph Caldwell, stated in his final report that the extremely large town dated from at least 800 AD and contained eight major mounds. The site was occupied by the ancestors of the Creek Indians or the Creek Indians until at least 1700 AD or later. At the time of its abandonment by the Creeks, all the buildings were burned, which probably indicated an attack by enemies. Sometime later after its abandonment, a small village composed of crude round huts was erected in one section of the original town. The historical Cherokee village of Tugaloo appears to have been a small village containing log houses that was built near the bank of the Tugaloo River, not on the island where the mounds are located.

Contemporary Georgia History books

The Georgia history books available to the general public also ignore the Colonial Era maps and the findings of professional archaeologists. Many make statements that go even farther into fiction than the historical markers.

New Georgia Encyclopedia

The New Georgia Encyclopedia is considered to be the most comprehensive and accurate overview of Georgia history. First published in 2004, the NGE was the first state encyclopedia to be created exclusively for publication online. Unlike Wikipedia, this encyclopedia contains original articles that are signed by the authors. Also, committees of recognized experts govern the contents of articles. This is in strong contrast to Wikipedia, where anonymous persons of unknown credentials, and often living in a foreign country, have dictatorial control over the content of American history articles. New Georgia Encyclopedia is a program of the Georgia Humanities Council in partnership with the University of Georgia Press, the University System of Georgia/GALILEO, and the Office of the Governor.

Unfortunately, despite these extensive quality controls, the New Georgia Encyclopedia's article on the history of the Georgia Mountains essentially parroted the false history of the Southern Highlands that has been aggressively promoted by the Eastern Band of Cherokee Indians in North Carolina since the early 1990s. Museums, archaeologists and government agencies are under constant pressure by EBC cultural officials to eliminate the word "Creek Indian" from museum exhibits and publications. The reason why will be explained later. The following are excerpts from that article.

NGE: "As carriers of epidemic diseases, Hernando de Soto and other Spanish explorers who visited the north Georgia mountains during the sixteenth century were directly responsible for the decline and eventual demise of the Mississippians. Within a century after Spanish contact, the Mississippians had all but vanished from the region."

No contemporary scholar believes that Hernando de Soto's Expedition traveled through the heart of the Georgia Mountains. The de Soto Expedition did cross the future state diagonally from south to east in the spring of 1540, then passed southward through the Great Appalachian Valley in extreme northwest Georgia during the summer of 1540, but it intentionally bypassed Georgia's major mountain ranges.

Until the late 1980s, Cherokee leaders consistently stated that the Cherokees originated in the Midwest, never built mounds and entered western North Carolina about the same time that South Carolina was being settled. At that point in time, a group of North Carolina archaeologists began promoting a new history of the Cherokees that described them as indigenous to North Carolina and full participants in the Mississippian mound building culture. Cherokee cultural leaders began claiming that their ancestors had built most of the mounds in the Southeast, were the first people in the world to cultivate corn, beans and squash, plus were the ancestors of the Mayas and Aztecs.

The relatively few mounds in western North Carolina were labeled the "Appalachian Mississippian Tradition," by North Carolina archeologists. Other archaeologists went along with that label, since it seemed quite appropriate.

In the three decades since the Appalachian Mississippian cultural label was created, however, North Carolina archaeologists have constantly pressured to extend the Appalachian Mississippian label to a broad swath of the Southeast that include Moundville, AL, Etowah Mounds, GA, Ocmulgee Mounds, GA, a cluster of mounds around Nashville, TN and many ancient towns sites in South Carolina. They have inserted that interpretation in as many online references as possible. Extending that line of illogic, the EBC and North Carolina archaeologists are gradually shifting the public's perception to conclude that, if the Cherokees were a Mississippian Culture, and all the other mound building peoples are extinct, then they are the sole descendants of the Mississippian Culture.

The next excerpt makes several statements that are not backed by either European maps or colonial archives:

Section of NGE entitled, **"Cherokee Mountains"**

NGE: "By 1700 the Cherokee Indians had located numerous villages in the mountains of Georgia and, like the Mississippians before them, grew corn and beans in the river bottoms and hunted large and small mammals in the near and distant forest." (grammatical errors are in the NGE)

The North Georgia Mountains were never called the Cherokee Mountains. English speakers called them the Appalachian or Blue Ridge Mountains. French and Spanish speakers called them the Apalache Mountains. The word Cherokee does not appear on any map or colonial archive until 1717. No map shows a Cherokee village in Georgia until 1725. Until after the American Revolution, Cherokee occupation in Georgia was limited to the extreme northeastern tip of the state. At the onset of the American Revolution, British military authorities estimated that there were about 200 Cherokees in the Province of Georgia, which then included the territory of Alabama and Mississippi.

NGE: "By 1716 regular trade was occurring between the Cherokees of the mountains and the Europeans living on the Atlantic Coast. Hunting and trapping for deer and beaver soon became a preoccupation of Cherokee men who thought that European weapons might give them an advantage over neighboring tribes. The fur trade reached its peak in the 1750s, as most Cherokee villages were becoming extremely dependent on European goods for sustenance. By 1760, buffalo and elk began to disappear entirely from the Georgia mountains. Bear and deer populations also suffered greatly, not only due to indiscriminate hunting practices but also because of the increasing number of open-range livestock in the mountains that competed with these animals for acorns and chestnuts. " (grammatical and spelling errors are in the NGE)

The year 1716 was at the most desperate stage of the Yamassee War. In late 1715, the Cherokees along with many other Southeastern tribes murdered all white traders in their midst. The Cherokees changed sides to the British in 1716, but at that time, bloody warfare between the Native American allies and the British colonists was going on throughout South Carolina. The Cherokees had murdered 32 Creek chiefs in their sleep at a diplomatic conference in 1716. This precipitated a 40 year long war between the Creeks and Cherokees. The Creeks eventually won, but the borderlands between the two tribes in the North Georgia Mountains remained a killing field.

NGE: "The introduction of livestock to the Georgia mountains eventually resulted in the clearing of canebrakes and the extermination of wild pea vines and strawberries from the forest floor. The changing composition of the mountain ecosystem had a profound effect on Cherokee culture. By 1800 the dress of a Cherokee man resembled that of a southern gentleman squire." (grammatical and spelling errors are in the NGE)

During the 40 years of the Creek-Cherokee War, very few people lived in the Northeast and North Central Georgia Mountains. There was a large, fortified Upper Creek town at the confluence of the Nottely River and Coosa Creek, which made life miserable for Cherokees on the Hiwassee River. There were two or three small villages in the Nacoochee Valley, which, for unknown reasons, the Creeks seldom bothered. There were Creeks and members of some allied tribes in small villages around Dahlonega, which also seemed to be off the main warpath.

Relatively large numbers of Creeks and Chickasaws continued to live in the Great Appalachian Valley of northwestern Georgia during the first ¾ of the 18th century. The lands there had been cultivated for at least 1000 years. Until after the American Revolution, the Cherokees only occupied three tiny hamlets on the extreme northeastern corner of Georgia. The first "Cherokees" to enter the heart of the mountains in 1776 were white British subjects with Native American wives. The men were Neutrals or Tories, who wanted to avoid being caught up in the Revolution. The wives could have been from any of several tribes. James Adair's wife was a Chickasaw.

When given the Upper Creek and Chickasaw lands in northwest Georgia in 1785, thousands of Cherokees poured into the long cultivated lands of the Great Appalachian Valley. However, even then, their population density was sparse. The maximum Cherokee populations of the two most densely populated counties, Bartow and Gordon, was only around 1200 people each. The more mountainous counties had maximum populations ranging from 150 to 300 Cherokees at the time of the Trail of Tears.

Between 1800 and 1832 a tiny minority of mixed blood Cherokees became slave-owning planters and wealthy. The mixed blood Cherokee planters did mimic the lifestyles of white planters. However, the vast majority of Cherokees remained dirt poor.

As any farmer or mountain boy would know, such plants as wild strawberries, river cane, wild peas, wild plums, persimmons, crabapples and pawpaws do NOT grow in the dense forests of the Georgia Mountains. There is too little sunshine and the soil is extremely acidic. These feral plants grow on fallow land or along the borders between cultivated lands and streams or roads. The Creek Indians intentionally established large expanses of strawberries on former cornfield plots that had been drained of nitrogen. They planted roots of three sizes of river cane between fields and streams to both ensure a ready supply of cane for arrows, spears, pipes and furniture . . . yes furniture . . . and also create a natural impenetrable wall to keep enemies out of villages.

The landscape that the first Europeans encountered in Georgia was an artificial one. It was the LACK of cultivation and crop rotation that caused the disappearance of many feral plants in the valleys of northern Georgia. One Creek town at the edge of the Cohutta Mountains, Kusa, had more residents in 1540, than the entire Cherokee Nation in 1832. The Cherokees had only been farmers a generation or two when they entered

24

Georgia in the late 1700s. They lacked the population to fully occupy the valleys as the ancestors of the Creeks had done. In response, Mother Nature began returning under-populated regions into their original ecology. It was the gold-mining, timber cutting and intensive livestock browsing of the white settlers who followed the Cherokees that radically changed the mountain's ecology for the worse.

The Georgia Studies Textbook – Carl Vinson Institute of Government

Currently, Georgia history is primarily taught to Middle School students via two certified textbooks and supplementary classroom aids. The more popular of the books is the Georgia Studies Textbook. This book says nothing about the period in the Georgia Mountains between 1600, when mound building ceased, and 1794, when the Cherokees were given most of northwestern Georgia as a sovereign territory. The book relies on articles in the New Georgia Encyclopedia, such as just discussed, to supplement the main text.

"The earliest Europeans in North America, the Spanish, never established any permanent settlements within the region that would become Georgia, as they did in Florida and along the Gulf Coast."

So that is what 99% of the citizens of Georgia believe. If their textbooks say so, it must be true. In Chapter Two, the reader will be introduced to a preponderance of French, Spanish, plus even British maps and archives that prove that Europeans were living in the Southern Appalachians for at least a century before there was even such a word as Cherokee.

Mahala Bone
A Young Creek Woman

CHAPTER TWO

La Historia Escondida
The Hidden History

The Hidden History

French and Dutch maps from the Colonial Period provide the names of ethnic groups within the interior of the Southeast, while they are generally absent from British maps before 1755. Several of the French maps even give the specific names of towns. Despite the fact that these maps were available at the Library of Congress throughout the 20th Century, and at the Hargrett Rare Map Collection at the University of Georgia Library for the past two decades, they were ignored by Late 20th century anthropologists and historians, when the "New Appalachian History" was fabricated.

Also inexplicable were the omissions of Virginia, British, French and Spanish archives concerning the Appalachian region during the late 1500s and 1600s. These documents contain the eyewitness accounts of travelers or traders in the Appalachian Region. They have been published for up to 425 years. The early ones only mention Muskogean Native Americans living in the region. Those in the 17th century describe Spanish, Portuguese, Jewish and African colonists also living in the region. A University of North Carolina history professor even went to the extreme of changing the name of an indigenous tribe that occupied northeast Tennessee and southwest Virginia from a branch of the Creeks to Cherokee, when he republished an account of a visit by a small group of Virginians to the Southern Highlands in 1673.

Maps of the Southern Highlands

1572 – 1684: All European maps showed northern Georgia and western North Carolina occupied by the Apalache Kingdom, a progenitor of the Creek Confederacy. At this time, the Georgia Mountains were the heart of the Creek-speaking peoples, whose territory stretched from southwestern Virginia (Tamahiti) to south-central Georgia (Tamatli) to the confluence of the Chattahoochee and Flint Rivers (Apalachicola.)

1684 – Jean Baptiste Franquelin: Franquelin's map of North America provides the names of the major towns in northern Georgia along the Chattahoochee River, plus the Upper Tennessee River in present day Tennessee. The dominant ethnic group in eastern Tennessee was the Caskenampo, which is a Koasati and Itsate Creek word meaning "Many Warriors." All the town names in northern Georgia were recognizable Creek words. Another interesting detail of this map is that in the 1680s the Apeka Creeks (Abeica ~ Abikara) were located on what appears to be the Chestatee River, east of Dahlonega, GA in the early 1680s. Their original location was on the French Broad River near its confluence with the Holston River in northeastern Tennessee.

1693 – Robert Morden: This map showed a single town, Apalache, in the Nacoochee Valley of Georgia. It appears to be the Spanish mining village that was observed by a British army scouting party about that same time in history. Apalache was the name of a branch of the Creek Indians that occupied much of the Southern Highlands in the 1500s and 1600s. The Appalachian Mountains got their name from this tribe. The Cherokees are not mentioned on this map.

1701 – Guilluam DeLisle - *Carte Du Mexique et de la Floride des Terres Angloises et des Isles Antilles du Cours et des Environs de la Riviere Mississipi*: DeLisle showed the Mountain Apalache to occupy the heart of the Georgia Mountains, the Upper Georgia Piedmont and the Hiwassee River Valley in western North Carolina. From 1701 to 1763 French maps showed most of northwestern Georgia and all of southeastern Tennessee to be Kusate territory. The Kusate were the descendants of the great town of Kusa, visited by Hernando de Soto in 1540. DeLisle's map showed that the Etowah River Valley in north-central and northwest Georgia was occupied by the Conchakee Creeks. The Conchakee were a part of the kingdom of Apalache. The province of Apalache was now located in the Georgia Piedmont, where the Apalachee River now flows.

Between 1684 and 1701, the Kofitachete (a non-Muskogean tribe with a Creek name) had relocated from south-central Tennessee in the Cumberland Plateau to the mountainous section of western North Carolina adjacent to the South Carolina line – roughly in the vicinity of Franklin, Highlands and Cashiers. Kofitachete is an Itsate-Creek word meaning "Mixed Ancestry People."

Several specific towns were labeled on the Upper Tennessee and Little Tennessee Rivers in DeLisle's map. The name that he called the Upper Tennessee was Caskinampo as in Franquelin's map. All of the town names were Muskogean words. Both this map and Franquelin's map mentioned the town, Tali, which was also visited by Hernando de Soto. DeLisle's map showed the Little Tennessee River in the Smoky Mountains of North Carolina being lined in succession by villages of the Talassee and Tuskegee Creeks, then farther eastward into North Carolina by Shawnee villages. He showed another large concentration of Shawnee villages on the middle Savannah River, both in present day Georgia and South Carolina.

1718 – Guilluam DeLisle - *Carte de la Louisiane et du Cours du Mississippi*: This was the first European map to mention the Cherokee Indians. DeLisle called them "Les Charaqui." The first mention of Charakee in the South Carolina archives was in 1717. The main Cherokee villages were located on the Holston, Nolichucky and Lower French Broad Rivers in northeastern Tennessee. The eight allied villages on the headwaters of the Savannah River were also labeled Charaqui. East central and southeast Tennessee were still occupied by Muskogean towns. The Little Tennessee River was still Muskogean territory in 1718 and served by French traders.

There were major changes on the 1718 DeLisle Map. The Apalache had moved south of the Georgia Mountains. The Georgia Mountains were controlled by the Kusate. The Koweta had moved into northeast Georgia. The Konchakee remained in the Etowah Valley.

Branches of the Muskogeans, by 1718 had moved southwestward out of the western North Carolina Mountains. These included the Chiaha, Tuskegee and Talassee. This probably reflected the initial phase of the Creek-Cherokee War, when 32 Creek peace chiefs and war chiefs were murdered in their sleep at diplomatic conference with the Cherokees. At that time, the word "Creek Indian" did not exist, however. The Cofitachete's were no longer mentioned on the map, but western North Carolina was left blank.

1725 – John Herbert – *Map of South Carolina*: This famous document marks the first time that actual "Charokee" villages were named on a European map. Earlier in the year, Colonel George Chicken had met with leaders of at least 14 bands of Natives at what is now Franklin, NC. He persuaded them to band together to form a tribe. He also wanted them to elect a "king" to facilitate relations with Great Britain.

In 1725, the Cherokees were called Charokees. Most of the villages were concentrated on the Tuckasegee River, where in 1718, Guilluam DeLisle had located the Cofitachete. No Charokee villages were shown on the Nolichucky and Holston Rivers, where DeLisle had shown their main concentration. The Tennessee River was labeled "The Hogeloge River, known to the Charokees as the Callimako River. The Hogeloge were a branch of the Yuchi. Surprisingly, they were the occupants of Tugaloo Island at the headwaters of the Savannah River, not Charokees. The diplomatic conference in which 32 Creek leaders were murdered had been held at Tugaloo. Perhaps at that time it was considered a neutral, Yuchi village.

There is something very odd about this initial map of the Cherokee Tribe. At least half of the village names are Muskogean words. All of the villages within the boundaries of modern South Carolina are standard Creek town names.

Unlike the French and Spanish maps of the period, the British map contains very little ethnic information on northern Georgia and southeastern Tennessee. At the headwaters of the Chattahoochee River are shown the Charokee villages of Chotee (Chote) and Nougouche (Nokose.) These are both Itsate Creek words. Along the Tallulah River near the present South Carolina line are show the Charokee villages of Teacone, Sokele and Carasere. The Sokele were once a very powerful Muskogean tribe in South Carolina.

1738 – Emmanuel Bowen – *Map of North and South Carolina*: This map shows numerous Cherokee villages in western North Carolina, plus along the Upper Tennessee and Little Tennessee River. However, it does not show any Cherokee villages in either northern Georgia or northwestern South Carolina.

1745 – Nicholas Sanson - *Map of North America*: This map shows all of the Chattahoochee, Flint and Suwanee River Basins as belonging to Spain. All Native villages in present day Georgia are either Creek or Apalache. The Mountain Apalache are shown to now live in southeast Georgia.

1754 – Emmanuel Bowen – *A New Map of Georgia*: This map shows no Cherokees living south of what is now the Georgia-North Carolina line. The Creek Indians occupy most of Georgia, while their kin, the Mountain Apalache, had moved from the mountains to southeastern Georgia. Both ethnic groups were allies of the Colony of Georgia and generally hostile to South Carolina.

At the time, South Carolina claimed all of Northern Georgia. In fact, most everybody else including the King of Great Britain assumed that northern Georgia was South Carolina. However, Georgia aggressively made treaties with the Creeks and Cherokees that ceded land to Georgia, not to South Carolina. The controversy would not be settled until 1785.

The Georgia Mountains are covered with the label, "*A fine, Fertile country by all accounts.*" Another, larger note diagonally crosses the western end of North Carolina and the northeastern tip of Georgia. It states, "*Deserted Cherakee Settlements.*"

1755 – John Mitchell – *Map of North America*: Typical of this situation was John Mitchell's Map of North America that was published in 1755. There was no ethnic information provided for northern Georgia. It contains the same two notes as the Bowen map. The Georgia Mountains are covered with the label, "*A fine, Fertile country by all accounts.*" Another, larger note diagonally crosses the western end of North Carolina and the northeastern tip of Georgia. It states, "*Deserted Cherakee Settlements.*" The Cherokees were not living in Georgia during that era. The fact that maps published between 1738 and 1755 show no Cherokees in Georgia suggests that the Creek-Cherokee War forced the Cherokees to retreat northward far sooner than current history textbooks suggest.

1763 – 1776: After the France ceded all of North America to Great Britain, colonial officials held a series of treaty conferences with the Southeastern tribes. The Cherokees were allowed to return to the lands they had lost in northeastern Georgia, but a buffer was put between them and the Koweta Creeks, who had wreaked such havoc in the Cherokee Nation in 1754. The Creek villages were to stay south of the Broad River. Small independent Creek tribes from South Carolina, such as the Eno, Cousaw, Etowaw and Tanasa were settled in the Georgia Mountains in between the Cherokee villages and the Koweta Creek villages. The Upper Creeks continued to occupy the remainder of northern Georgia.

1776 – G. Romain – Map of the Southern Provinces for British Army showed three Cherokee villages in northeastern Georgia; Noguchee, Chote and Soque. In 1773 the Creeks and Cherokees had signed a treaty giving up their claims to the eastern portion of northeastern Georgia, northward to the headwaters of the Savannah River. The Creeks continued to occupy a corridor northward to what is now Clarksville, GA and the southern edge of the Nacoochee Valley.

1780 – An anonymous map of the Province of Georgia produced by the British Army in 1780 went no further west than the headwaters of the Chattahoochee. Only one Cherokee village remained in northeast Georgia, Noguchee. The British Army estimated that there were approximately 200 Cherokees in the entire Province of Georgia.

There was a note that lands west of the Chattahoochee River were occupied by the Upper Creeks, but no map showing specific village locations. Apparently, the Chattahoochee River headwaters were the north-south dividing line between the two tribes. The southern boundary of the Cherokees in northeast Georgia was Yonah Mountain, which overlooks the Chattahoochee River in the Nacoochee Valley. South of there was a neutral band of hunting territory. South of the Broad River was Koweta Creek territory.

1795 – Russell: *Map of the United States of America and Possessions of the British Empire in North America*: In 1785 the Creek Confederacy agreed to give up its claim to most of northwestern and north central Georgia in return for being "given" most of Alabama. The Chickasaws occupied a significant section on the western side of northwest Georgia, but were not given a say in the matter. Their lands were given to the Cherokees also. These ceded lands were initially designated as Cherokee hunting lands. In 1794, the Cherokees gave up the northeastern tip of Georgia, but were "given" their hunting lands as their new home. The State of Georgia bitterly protested this treaty.

1823 – *Map of Georgia and Alabama*: In the Treaty of Fort Jackson in 1814, the Creeks were forced to cede all of their lands in southwest Georgia. This region was occupied by Itsate-speaking Creeks, who had been allies of the United States in the Red Stick War. In 1818 the Creeks ceded a narrow corridor of land extending northward along the east side of the Chattahoochee River to Clarksville, GA. By this time, only mixed blood, fully assimilated Creeks lived in that region.

There would be no map that accurately portrayed the locations of northern Georgia's rivers until 1838. The mountain ridges would not be accurately mapped until acquired by the U. S. Forest Service in the mid-20ᵗʰ century.

Eyewitness accounts and refugees seeking asylum

1492 – King Ferdinand and Queen Isabel expelled all Jews, who were not willing to convert to Catholicism. Some of these Jews went to Muslim countries, where they would be tolerated as long as they paid a tax for not being Muslim. The majority initially moved to Portugal, Brazil, France, England, the Netherlands and Germany. The Netherlands eventually received more Jewish immigrants than any other country. Many Sephardic Jews prospered in the Protestant Netherlands. They became known as *svart duits* (Black Dutch). Over time, they adopted Dutch as their first language, but continued to use either Hebrew or Ladino (a Spanish-Arabic-Hebrew dialect) in their homes and religious services.

1492 – It has been estimated that at least 73% of the sailors in Columbus' fleet were Conversos, Cryptic Jews or Moriscos. [1] These ethnic groups continued to be disproportionately represented among ships' crews and colonists for the next century. There is substantial evidence that Columbus, Cristobal Colon, was from a Converso family in Barcelona. Colon was the name of a prominent Jewish Converso family living there. Almost all of Columbus' writings are in Catalan, the language of Barcelona.

Some of the most important members of Columbus' crew were Sephardic Jews. These men included: Roderigo Sanchez De Segovia (Queen Isabel's Inspector), Doctor Marco (Surgeon), Maestre Bernal (Physician), Luis De Torres (Interpreter) and Roderigo De Triana, the first sailor to sight land.

1497 – Under pressure from his new Asturian wife and the Spanish state, King Manuel I of Portugal rescinded his tolerance of Jews and demanded that they convert. [2] The two brothers of Christopher Columbus gave many Jews asylum on the islands of Cuba and Dominica; the Bahama Islands and the south central coast of Puerto Rico.

1506 – The massacre of over 2,000 Jews in Lisbon, Portugal caused a mass out-migration of Jews to the Americas. [3]

1526 – Approximately 80 North African and African slaves escaped the San Miguel de Gualdape Colony on Sapelo Island, GA. They made their way to the interior and disappeared from history. [4]

34

1530 – Cryptic Jews began to settle in large numbers on the island of Jamaica. The governor of Jamaica practiced a "Don't ask, don't tell" policy toward the Jewish colonists. [5]

1536 – The Portuguese Inquisition was established. This caused many descendants of Spanish Jews, who had taken refuge in Portugal, to leave the country. Many went to the New World. [6]

1540 – Several Iberian and African members of the De Soto Expedition went AWOL after falling for pretty Native women in northern Georgia. It is quite probable that the de Soto Expedition included several Conversos and Moriscos in addition to the Muslim African slaves mentioned in its chronicles.

1554 – French pirates began to operate off the coast of Spain and increasingly in the West Indies after Spain openly became involved in the Catholic League's war on the French Huguenots. [7] Most of these pirates were either Protestants or Sephardic Jews. Through the decades that followed, Sephardic Jews living in Jamaica and the Bahamas were increasingly active in attacking Spanish ships. Spanish Catholics on these ships were usually either killed or left on small uninhabited islands. The Protestant, Orthodox Christian and Muslim naval slaves were freed. It is believed that these freed slaves were sometimes dropped off on the coast of the Southeast, since until the early 1600s there were no Protestant colonies in the Americas other than Dutch Brazil.

1566 – Six French Huguenot men, who survived the massacre of Fort Caroline on September 21, 1565, made their way up the Altamaha and Oconee Rivers to the Kingdom of Apalache's capital in the Georgia Mountains. The town was probably located in the Choestoe Community in Union County. The king of Apalache gave them asylum. The Frenchmen married Apalache wives and spent the rest of their life there.

1566-1567 – Captain Juan Pardo led a large company of Spanish soldiers on an expedition through the Southern Appalachians. [8] The Native provinces all spoke Muskogean languages and were still thriving. Pardo intended to travel all the way to Kusa, but was tipped off that a combined army from several towns planned to ambush him on the road to Kusa that passed through the heart of the Apalache (Georgia) Mountains.

Captain Juan Pardo built five forts to protect the route between Santa Elena, SC on the coast and the gold and silver deposits in the mountains of Georgia and North Carolina. Most of the enlisted men were Basques, Moriscos or Conversos. Pardo was a Spanish ethnic term in the 1400s and 1500s. It could be roughly translated as "half-breed," a term to describe the offspring of marriages between lighter skinned Christians and dark-skinned North Africans.

1567 – All but one man of the five garrisons that Captain Juan Pardo established in the Southern Appalachians and Piedmont disappeared. [9] Spanish officials were told by friendly Indians that they had been massacred, but this was never confirmed.

1568-1584 – With the full knowledge of the Governor of La Florida, a steady stream of Spanish traders traveled covertly to the Apalache to trade European crafted items for gold, silver, copper, sapphires, rubies and diamonds. [10] Almost all Spanish traders were forbidden to enter the inner sanctum of the Apalache in the Nottely River Valley. Trading probably occurred at villages located near Dahlonega, GA, Helen, GA and six miles north of Athens, GA.

Most Spaniards, who attempted to hike into the Nottely Valley over the gap at Blood Mountain, were killed on sight. Sixteenth century Spanish armor has been found near US Hwy. 19-129, south of Blood Mountain, which follows the old Native American "Great White Path." The White Path is mentioned in both the Rochefort book and the "Migration Legend of the Kashita People. [11]

1571 – Battle of Lepanto – This great naval victory of the Holy League over the Ottoman Empire, resulted in the freeing of 12,000 Christian galley slaves and the capture of about 10,000 prisoners-of-war.[12] At least a third of the prisoners were also Christians, but unless they were Catholics from the Balkan countries, they were made into galley slaves. Captured Jewish soldiers and sailors were also enslaved. During the late 1500s and early 1600s, prisoner-of-war slaves represented a significant percentage of personnel on Spanish warships.

1580 – Spain and Portugal were united under the rule of the King of Spain in 1580. [13] Immediately, Spanish Inquisition officials intensified the investigations and torture of Christianized Jews, who they suspected were practicing Jewish traditions in secret. This began a period when large numbers of Conversos, Moriscos and Crypto-Jews migrated from Portugal to remote Spanish colonies such as La Florida and Nuevo Leon in northern Mexico. The records of the commoners who migrated from Iberia to La Florida no longer survive. However, even if the names were known, it would probably be difficult to determine which were Conversos or Crypto-Jews.

1585 – Archaeologists working on proto-Creek town sites in northwestern Georgia have repeatedly discovered that all the major towns in that region were suddenly abandoned at some time in the period between 1585 and 1600. Radiocarbon dating cannot be more precise.

1589 – Roanoke Colony survivors arrived in the Nacoochee Valley in the Georgia Mountains, according to Eleanor Dare stones. [14] The Chattahoochee River begins a few miles north of the Nacoochee Valley.

c. 1590 – In 1890, a 400+ foot long, sloping shaft mine was discovered in Mitchell County, NC. [15] Mitchell contains some of North Carolina's most rugged mountains and is northwest of Asheville. A tree growing up through the shaft of the mine was found to be 300 years old.

1599 – Eleanor Dare died of natural causes in the Nacoochee Valley, according to her grave marker. [16] Before dying she bore several children with her Apalache husband. Apparently, most or all of the Roanoke Colony survivors married Apalache spouses in order secure acceptance in the province.

1601 -The governor of Florida received repeated reports of a large band of white men on horseback repeated being seen in the Georgia Piedmont and mountains. [17] An expedition to central Georgia was dispatched under the command of Juan de Lara in 1602.

1603 – Persia invaded eastern Turkey, which was predominantly Christian. [18] In fact, at that time, over a third of the population of the Ottoman Empire was Christian. After Persia captured the region around Mount Ararat and the nation of Georgia, approximately a half million Christian civilians were killed and at least another 300,000 were evicted from the region. The Christians were unwelcome in western Turkey. They were forced to wander the Mediterranean Basin until finding somewhere that would accept them. It is believed that many of these refugees ended up in the Americas.

1609 – Approximately, 350,000 Moriscos (nominally converted Muslims) and Conversos (nominally converted Jews) were expelled from Spain and Portugal after a Morisco Rebellion. [19] A significant percentage of these refugees were devout, practicing Christians, who would be executed if they went to a Muslim country.

1610 – Cartagena, Colombia probably had the largest Jewish population in the Americas until this year. [20] Many families in the Jewish community had grown wealthy from owning merchant fleets, operating the African slave trade, and working African slaves in gold and silver mines. Cartagena was one of two cities where the Spanish Crown allowed African slaves to be sold.

The Spanish Inquisition arrived in Cartagena without warning. Very quickly many of the wealthiest families who were more visible in their Jewish practices, left the city for parts unknown. Other Jewish families assumed that by attending Mass and confession regularly, they would be safe. However, the Inquisition went after some of the most respected Jewish leaders and intellectuals in Cartagena a few years later. Their torture and public burning provoked a tidal wave of Jewish out-migration.

1615 – A Sephardic Jewish couple made their marriage legal in the absence of a rabbi by carving "PRE DARMOS CASADA – SEP 15, 1615" on a boulder at 5400 feet above sea level on Hoopers Bald, NC in the Great Smoky Mountains. [21] The Ladino words mean "Prayer we will give Married, September

PRE DARMOS CASADA

PRE DARMOS CASADA SEP 15 . 1615

Richard Thornton

This inscription clearly shows the presence of Sephardic
Jews form Portugal and Spain in the Southern Highlands in
the 17th Century.

15, 1615. "Pre" was the word used for prayer by Sephardic Jews while Spanish Catholics used the word "suplicación."

1622 – According to Charles de Rochefort, English colonists settled in a location near the capital of Apalache, instead of Virginia, because there was a sudden and violent rebellion among the Powhatan Indians. [22] The king of Apalache allowed them to build a Protestant chapel there.

1624-1628 – Repeated rumors of English-speaking white men in the northern part of Georgia caused the governor of Florida to dispatch at least five reconnaissance expeditions into the northern Coastal Plain between 1624 and 1628. [23] Two of the reconnaissance missions were under the command of Ensign Pedro de Torres. De Torres' parties penetrated as far as central South Carolina.

1643 – Florida sent missionaries and surveyors up the Chattahoochee River as far as its source near Helen, GA. [24] A mission was established on the Chattahoochee River near present day Columbus, GA. According to Charles de Rochefort, this expedition marked the beginning of increased Spanish influence and immigration in the Southern Appalachians.

1646 – Governor Benito Ruíz de Salazar Vallecilla established a trading post on the headwaters of the Chattahoochee River in the Nacoochee Valley. [25] The purpose of this trading post was to initiate the deerskin trade with the various branches of the Muskogeans, Shawnees and Yuchi living in the Southern Highlands.

The village that developed around it was called Apalache on the 1693 John Morden map. It appears to be approximately where Sautee, GA and the Kenimer Mound are located. A polyglot community of gold miners occupied Apalache in addition to their Native spouses and mestizos.

1646 – A pack mule trail was constructed between St. Augustine, San Mateo on the St. Johns River, present day Waycross, present day Dublin, present day Athens and the Nacoochee Valley. It was later extended to the Tennessee River and probably the Holston River. According to Charles de Rochefort, the Spanish also built a Catholic mission next to the trading post, but to date, we cannot find any record of it.

The Spanish trade route, known as the La Cota Trail, was still in use in the late 1700s. The extension of the trail between the Nacoochee Valley and the Tennessee River was then known as the Unicoi Trail. In North Carolina, it is also known as the Joe Brown Turnpike; in Tennessee, the Unicoi Turnpike.

1646 – At the start of conflict in 1641 between the English Parliament and King Charles I, the aristocratic Bland family relocated to Spain. [26] They were apparently Roman Catholics, since Protestants and Jews were forbidden from living in Spain or its colonies. Despite being English, they prospered from trading activities associated with the Canary Islands.

In 1646, Edward Bland sailed to Virginia. He immediately traveled to a unknown location in the Southern Appalachians for reasons never publicly stated. It is quite probable that his covert trip involved a visit to the new trading post in the Nacoochee Valley or perhaps visits with Spanish miners in the Southern Highlands.

1650 – Rabbi Manassah Ben Israel, Chief Rabbi of Amsterdam recorded an intriguing story in his book *Mikveh Yisrael*, written in 1650. [27] He related a conversation that he had with a Jewish Dutch explorer of the Americas. The explorer related how he made contact with some Native Americans in the Appalachian Mountains, but after trying to communicate with them in every possible European language, he had no success. Being a Jew, as was his first mate, these two began to talk amongst themselves in Late Medieval Hebrew. To his utter amazement, upon hearing him speak Hebrew to his first mate, the Native American chief responded in kind and stated, "Shema Yisrael."

1651 – A Mr. Brigstock (probably Richard Brigstock) of Barbados toured the Kingdom of Apalache in northern Georgia. [28] He reported to a friend, the Rev. Charles de Rochefort, that the Englishmen had settled in northern Georgia early in the 1600s and now were settling in large numbers in the region that is called northeastern Tennessee. He said that the southern part of Apalache was coming under increasing influence from Spanish immigrants.

1653 – A party of Virginians under the leadership of Francis Yeardley visited the principal chief of the Tuscarora in central North Carolina. [29] The chief told them that a wealthy Spaniard, thirty members of his family and seven Africans had lived in his village for seven years before moving westward.

1654 – Portugal captured the Dutch colony of Northern Brazil. All Jews were expelled. It is documented that at least one shipload of Portuguese Jewish refugees settled in New Amsterdam. By this time, Dutch ships were regularly trading with New Amsterdam and the English ports in Virginia. The ships could have easily dropped off refugees at remote locations.

1669 – Johann Lederer, a recent immigrant to Virginia from Germany, led a small exploration party southward along the Blue Ridge Mountain escarpment of North Carolina. [30] This was one of three journeys that he made to the west in search of a route to the Pacific Ocean. The map, which he prepared for his book on the journey, showed the southwest Virginia and NW North Carolina Mountains occupied solely by the Rickohocken Indians. The party turned around at the headwaters of the Keowee River. In the vicinity of the Keowee, Lederer sketched a man-made dam and pond. Lederer's map does not mention the Cherokees or Spanish settlers in the mountains.

1671 – Thomas Wood, Thomas Batt and Robert Fallon departed from Petersburg, VA to find a quicker route to the "South Sea" – presumably meaning the Gulf of Mexico. [31] Four days into the journey, a horse became lame. They hired a man that they described only as a "Portugal" to take the horse back to Petersburg. The location is now Brookneal, VA in the south-central part of the Commonwealth. What really stands out in this story was that the men did not consider it unusual to find a Portuguese man in the Virginia wilderness.

1673 – In June of 1673 the Marquette Expedition (French) encountered American Indians living at the confluence of the Ohio River and the Mississippi River, who had firearms, munitions, European tools and cloth. [32] The French could not determine the source of these European items, but did confirm that they did not come from direct trade with English, French or Spanish colonies. The Indians refused to divulge the source of the goods. The origins of these items seemed to have been from several countries.

1673 – In July of 1673, Robert Needham and Gabriel Arthur led a party from Petersburg, VA southwestward in attempt to open up trade contacts with large Indian towns located at the confluence of the Upper Tennessee and Little Tennessee River. [33] After Needham returned, Abraham Woods wrote a letter to John Richards, a financier in England that described the journey. It is quite possible that Abraham Woods was Jewish, since the use of Old Testament names only slowly received acceptance after the Protestant Reformation. Prior to then, all persons were given the names of saints. Richards is a typical English Jewish name, but not always.

The following are excerpts from the original letter written by Abraham Woods to John Richards, a merchant in England. Several versions of this letter are published on the internet which substitute the word "Charakee" for a Tamahiti, a branch of the Creeks. Most of these altered versions also leave out discussion of Spaniards living in what has long been assumed to be traditional Cherokee territory. (key words are emphasized)

"Eight dayes jorny down this river lives **a white people which have long beardes and whiskers** and weares clothing, and on some of ye other rivers lives a hairey people ..."

". . . and all ye wesocks children they take are brought up with them as ye **Ianesaryes** (Janessaries) are a mongst ye **Turkes.** this King came to my house upon ye 21st of June as you will heare in ye following discouerse."

"Ye prisoner relates that **ye white people have a bell which is six foot over which they ring morning and**

evening and att that time a great number of people congregate togather and talkes he knowes not what. **They have many blacks among them.**"

"Now after ye tumult was over they make preparation for to manage ye warr for that is ye course of theire liveing to forage robb and spoyle other nations and the king commands Gabriell Arther to goe along with a party that went to robb ye **Spanyarrd,** promising him that in ye next spring hee him selfe would carry him home to his master."

"They travelled eight days west and by south as he guest and came to a **town of negroes, spatious and great, but all wooden buildings** Heare they could not take anything without being spied. The next day they marched along by ye side of a **great carte path,** and about five or six miles as he judgeth came within **sight of the Spanish town**, walld about with brick and all brick buildings within. There he saw ye steeple where in hung ye bell which Mr. Needham gives relation of and harde it ring in ye evening."

"Well, shall now give a relation, what my man hath discovered in all ye time that Mr. James Needham left him att ye Tomahitans to ye 18th of June 74. which was ye daye Gabriell arived att my house in safety with a **Spanish Indian boy.**"

"Ye 7th day a **Spanniard in a gentille habitt**, accoutered with gunn, sword and pistol, one of ye Tomahittans espieing him att a distance crept up to ye path side and shot him to death."

"By this meanes wee know this is not ye river ye **Spanyards** live upon as Mr. Needham did thinke."

1674 – Henry Woodward traveled to a Westo town near where Augusta, GA is located today. [34] The name of the village was a word recorded by English speakers as being similar to Rickohocken. Woodward reported to the colonial authorities that there was a cluster of villages on the tributaries of the Savannah River that the Westo called Chorake, who were their enemies. Chorake is a Muskogee-Creek word that means "Splinter People."

1675 – In 1675 Pablo de Salazar, a government bureaucrat in Santo Domingo, wrote other officials to describe his concept of a Mexican Indian colony in the Florida Panhandle. [35] The plan was to bring Maya weavers and Mexican farmers to the region in order to pump up the colony and provide more militiamen for defending Florida against English and French incursions. **He stated that both the English and the French had been settling in the region north of Florida.** He also stated that the English were giving firearms to the Chichimeca Indians then training them in European military practices. He feared that the purpose of this military assistance was to dispatch them on slave raids to the Florida missions.

1684 – The towns of Tamasee, Okonee and Keowah on the headwaters of the Savannah River made a trade agreement with the governor of the Charlestown Colony.[36] Virtually all historical references refer to this as the first treaty with the Cherokee Indians. The word Cherokee is not mentioned. The first treaty with the Cherokee Tribe was in 1721. In this agreement, the governor agreed to allow traders to visit their towns.

Itza Maya Woman in Guatemala Highlands
Photo by Richard Thornton

1690s – Asheville's famous historian F. A. Sondley found archival evidence that Spaniards were living in large numbers on the Toe River in the North Carolina Mountains and Nolichucky River in extreme eastern Tennessee during the 1690s. [37] The Toe River flows into the Nolichucky River, which then flows into the French Broad River, which then joins the Holston River to form the Tennessee River. The Spruce Pine Mining District on the North Toe River is one of the richest deposits of precious stones in the world.

1690 – James Moore and Maurice Mathews attempted to prospect for gold in the Nacoochee Valley, but were turned away by what they thought were hostile Native Americans. [38] All references label these hostiles to be Cherokees. That is absolutely impossible. The Cherokees didn't exist in 1690 and they didn't capture the Nacoochee Valley from the Creeks until after they changed sides in the Yamasee War.

Moore and Mathews then took the Unaka Trail northward into what is now Clay and Cherokee Counties, North Carolina. Here they observed white men mining, probably in the Andrews Valley where there were silver deposits. All the men wore long beards. In the Europe of 1690, that would have been very *faux pas*, unless one was Jewish or an Irish/Scottish peasant.

Folklore called the local Natives, Cherokees, but in 1690 in Tomatla, North Carolina, they would have been Tamatli Creeks, speaking the Itsate Creek language. Even after the Cherokees took over, the large town kept the name, Tamatli. The local Natives were not considerable hosts. Several years later the locals told the British that they had killed the bearded miners; three years after Moore met them. The timing of the murders coincides with a British Army patrol that visited the Nacoochee Valley.

1690 –French engineers and traders explored and mapped the Little Tennessee River Basin in western North Carolina. They encountered a village that they said had to be seen to be believed. [39] It was a town of log cabins. It occupants had European beards, hair color and eyes. They spoke a broken form of Elizabethan English. The olive complexion of these mountaineers and past experience with Mediterranean traders led the French explorers to conclude they had found a colony of "Moors" in the New World of North America.

These hybrids may have been Sephardic Jews or they may have met people of mixed English-Native American heritage. As stated earlier, the king of Apalache allowed Englishmen to settle in the mountains.

1693 – A party of 20 Chorake leaders with Creek or English names from a cluster of towns at the headwaters of the Savannah River traveled to Charlestown to seek help in the return of their people, who had been captured in slave raids by the Savano, Kusaw and Esaw tribes. [40] Governor Ludwell offered to provide the group of towns with firearms and treat with them as a tribe. This is considered the beginning of the Cherokee Indians as a tribe, but the name "Cherokee" would not appear on maps for another 20 years.

1694 – An exploration party composed of British soldiers and their Native American guides from the Savannah Headwaters towns followed a trail to a vantage point overlooking the Nacoochee Valley. Presumably, this was on Tray Mountain. [41] The British observed many columns of smoke. They were told by their native guides that the smoke was produced by the gold smelters, being operated by Spanish gold miners. The British soldiers turned around and reported their discovery to government officials in Charleston. The report is in British colonial archives, but was left out of the history books.

1700 – In 1957 and 1958, University of Georgia archaeologist, Joseph Caldwell, led the excavation of the Tugaloo Site, a large proto-Creek town on an island in the Tugaloo River, upstream from the headwaters of the Savannah River. [42] In his final report, Caldwell stated that the town had been occupied by Creek Indians at least until 1700 AD. He could not be more accurate because of the imprecision of radiocarbon dating. He found that at some time in the very early 1700s the large Creek town had been burned. It was soon replaced by a small village with crude round houses.

1700 – Englishman, John Lawson, and some companions paddled up the Santee River to the Congoree River. They then paddled up the Congoree River to its headwaters. [43] From there they hiked southwestward along the edge of the Blue Ridge Mountains to the headwaters of the Keowee River. There, they stayed in the cabin of a friendly Keowee Indian. Most "Cherokee histories" change the word, Keowee, to Cherokee. Lawson's book never mentions the words Cherokee, Chorakee or Rickohocken. He also did not mention seeing any Portuguese, Spanish or Jewish colonists.

Lawson described the Keowee men as being extremely tall, plus they wore mustaches and turbans. This is exactly how de Soto described the men of the Oconee Province in Georgia. Islamic scholars cite these two descriptions as "proof" that the Creek Indians were Muslims. This is not the case. Creek men averaged a foot taller than 16th century Europeans and Arabs. Seven foot tall skeletons have been found in royal burials at Etowah Mounds and Ocmulgee. The Mayas and ancestors of the Creeks were wearing turbans and head bands long before Islam existed. The mustache was a symbol among all branches of the Creeks that a man had been in combat. Until the 1700s, Creek elders wore goatees, just like the customs of several ethnic groups in Mexico.

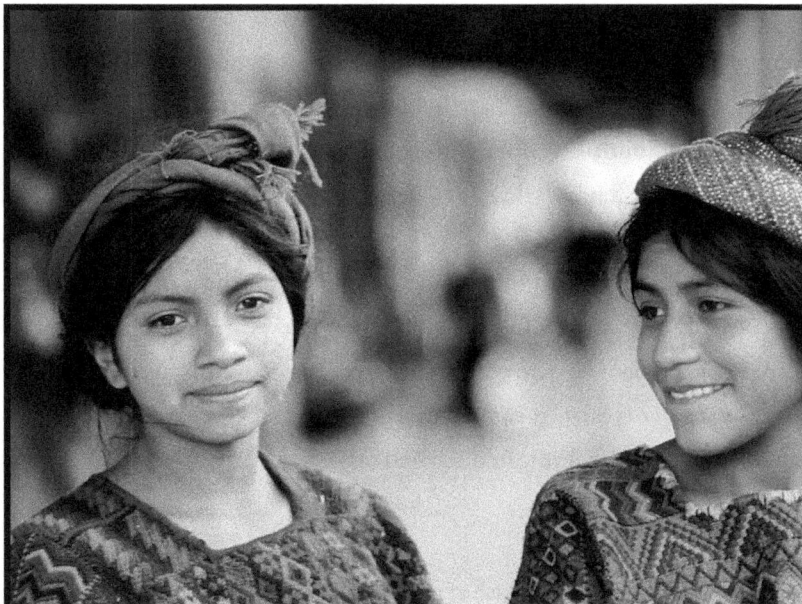

Itsa Maya Teens Wearing Turbans
Photo from Wikipedia Commons

Virtually all non-Muskogean anthropologists today assume that the Kiawee were always a division of the Cherokees and spoke an Algonquian language. They actually were a division of the Oconee-Creek Indians and called themselves the Kiale or Kiawa. Kiawah Island, SC once was their coastal trading center, but their mother town was on the Oconee River, where Watkinsville, GA is now located. Kialegi Tribal Town in Oklahoma is a direct descendant of these people. The Keowee in South Carolina, that helped form the original "Chorakee" alliance, were colonists of the main branch in Georgia.

1714 – In Cherokee tradition, the Cherokees made a surprise attack on Yuchi towns on the west side of the Hiwassee River as revenge for the murder of a Cherokee man and killed all the inhabitants. [44] Another version is that a trader named Wiggins was angry at the Yuchi because they caught him making a crooked trade and cut off an ear.

In fact, this was probably a military action instigated by the British against Native allies of the French in eastern Tennessee. The Wiggins story probably was a cover, because nothing came of the criminal charges that Wiggins supplied the Cherokees with muskets. The proto-Cherokees had muskets provided by the British, while the Yuchi's did not. The Yuchi's supposedly fought to the death from inside their public buildings.

1715 – A Jewish girl or woman named Liube carved her name and the date, 1715, on the Track Rock Petroglyphs between Blairsville, GA and Brasstown Bald Mountain. [45] Some of the bloodiest events of the Yamasee War occurred in 1715. Perhaps she was letting potential rescuers know that she was alive.

1716 – In the second phase of the Yamasee War, Chorake leaders in northwestern South Carolina invited leaders from Muskogean towns in western North Carolina and northern Georgia to Tugaloo in order to plan a joint attack on the South Carolina Colony. [46] Modern versions of the story label the Native American participants in this conference, the Cherokees and Creeks, but neither tribe existed in 1716.

A Chorake sorcerer named Charite Haggi informed the Chorake chiefs that the demons in the Sacred Fire at Tugaloo had told him that if the Chorake killed their guests and switched sides to the British, the Chorake would become a great people, who would conquer the entire Southeast. *Charate* means "Splinter People" in Itsate Creek. *Haggi* means "prophet" in Turkish. The Chorake leaders did as their conjurer told them. The Cherokee Alliance that resulted seemed invincible for two decades afterward, then was hit by one disaster after another.

1717 – First mention of Cherokee tribe: Within the minutes of the Colonial Council was a mention of a "Charakee Path" that led to a cluster of Native villages at the headwaters of the Savannah River. [47]

c. 1721 – A non-Cherokee man who had traveled south to join the Overhill Cherokees, was given the name, "White Owl." When he became a leader, he was given the name, "Attakullakulla" (*Probably Atta*

Kullak Ula.) British officials couldn't translate his name, but thought it might have something to do with wood, so they called him, "Little Carpenter." In 1997 author Brent Kennedy stated that his name was Turkish and meant, "Spiritual father of the Red Men." [48] Attakullakulla married a Natchez woman, captured on a slave raid, then later became the peace chief of the Cherokee Nation.

1745 – Cherokee Indians entered the Tuckasegee River Basin in present day Jackson County, NC for the first time. Sylva, the county seat of Jackson County, is only 16 miles from the North Carolina Reservation, but is separated from the reservation by mountains over a mile high. [49]

The Cherokees sent a report to colonial authorities in Charleston that they had not seen any American Indians, but there were several villages in the valley occupied by "white" families with skin the color of Indians. The men wore long beards and appeared to speak Spanish with each other. The houses were built out of logs and had arched windows. The Cherokees stated that these people "worshiped a book." Because the settlers were obviously not British, the Cherokees drove them out of the valley or killed those who resisted.

1775 – William Adair published his landmark book, **The History of the American Indians**. [50] A substantial portion of the book was composed of his arguments that the Southeastern Indians were the descendants of the Lost Ten Tribes of Israel. He had observed customs practiced by his Chickasaw wife, which seemed derived from Judaism. They may well have been. The Chickasaws were indigenous to eastern Tennessee, the northwestern tip of Georgia and northern Alabama. A Jewish female may have passed down certain ways of doing things to her daughters, and her daughters to their daughters.

John Adair stated in his book that several hundred Cherokees, living in the North Carolina Mountains, spoke an ancient Jewish language that was nearly unintelligible to Jews from England and Holland.

1780-1784 – While the Patriot cause in the Southern colonies seemed at its lowest ebb in 1780, former Shenandoah County, Virginia residents, Colonel John C. Tipton and Colonel John Sevier, began leading wagon trains of Shenandoah County residents down to what is now northeastern Tennessee, but was then North Carolina. [51] A wide range of rugged mountains would protect the pioneers from British Redcoats in the Carolina Piedmont. Most settlers went to what is now the Johnson City area.

On their first trip down to Tennessee, Tipton observed very old villages in SW Virginia and NE Tennessee that were occupied by Spanish speaking Jews. Tipton stated that the Jewish families appeared to make their living as gold and silver smiths. He could not figure out who they sold their products to. The Jewish settlers' command of English was so poor that they could not answer many of his questions.

Since passing through these villages, Colonel Sevier had always been curious about the people with olive complexions and black hair in northeastern Tennessee. [52] In 1784 he took a horseback ride across several counties along the northeastern tier of the Tennessee Territory, and encountered hundreds of people who appeared to be either of Spanish, Moorish or Jewish ancestry.

Sevier stumbled upon an entire community of these unusual people in the Newman's Ridge region of upper East Tennessee. After entering their village, he discovered that they spoke broken English. Unlike the Cherokees, these people identified themselves as "Porty-ghee" and said that they were Christians.

1828 – Laborers employed by South Carolina Senator John C. Calhoun discovered the well-preserved ruins of a mining village along Dukes Creek in the Nacoochee Valley of Georgia. [53] It was on land acquired by Calhoun for gold mining. The Georgia Gold Rush had just begun.

The miners uncovered the foundations of several log houses, plus what appeared to be the timber-lined shaft of a pit mine. They also found iron or steel tools and weapons that were typical of the 1600s. A Spanish cigar mold was also discovered. The artifacts were viewed and authenticated by anthropologist, Charles C. Jones, Jr. and described in his landmark book on the Indians of Georgia.

1913 – William Dockery of Marble, NC explored a 16th or 17th century mine shaft in nearby Tomatla, NC. [54] It was cribbed eight feet square every three feet by massive red oak girders and posts. Ancient Spanish iron tools were found in the mine, which Dockery explored for 65 feet into the tunnel. Nearby was the ruin of an ancient furnace. A Spanish coin mold was also found nearby. The presence of a coin mold suggests that at least some of the Spanish mining operations in the Southern Appalachians had the approval of government authorities in St. Augustine or that the miners were making counterfeit coins.

This location in the Andrews Valley is very significant. The mine was in the Snowbird Mountains where Juan Pardo found silver ore in 1567. The highway serving Tomatla is none other than U. S. 129 that connects the Little Tennessee River with the head of canoe navigation on the Oconee River in northeast Georgia. The Creek Indians called this route, the Great White Path. It went through Track Rock Gap.

1996 – Spanish and Native American glyphs were discovered on boulders near Nickajack Creek in Smyrna, GA. [55] They appeared to be a Spanish gold mine claim or else, a territorial claim by both the Spanish and their Native American allies. The glyphs have never been studied by an archaeologist.

A Spanish trading post or village may have been located at the confluence of Nickajack Creek and the Chattahoochee River. There is a designated archaeological zone at this location that has never been excavated by archeologists. In the state site files, it is called a Historic Cherokee village site. This label is entirely based on local folklore, because early white settlers found European artifacts around the site.

2012 – Melungeon researchers found extensive evidence of a community on the Pee Dee River in South Carolina composed of people of mixed Portuguese and Native American descent. [56] The Portuguese were probably Sephardic Jews from Portugal. Apparently, they arrived in the region in the early-to-mid 1600s, prior to the settlement of Charleston, SC. Currently the earliest known printed mention of these people is 1754. Their existence matches perfectly the 1654 eyewitness account of the Yeardley Expedition that said that extended "Spanish" families were migrating from the coast of the Carolinas to the mountains.

REFERENCES AND NOTES

1. Pachecker, Humphrey Humberto, **The Immigrant's Universe,** Xlibris, 2010, p. 27.

2. Benveniste, Arthur, "500th Anniversary of the Forced Conversion of the Jews of Portugal," Address at Sephardic Temple Tifereth Israel, Los Angeles, October,1997.

3. Ibid.

4. Swanton, John R., **Early History of the Creek Indians and their Neighbors, 1922**; p. 32-48.

5. Benveniste, Arthur, Ibid.

6. Ibid.

7. Plotkin, Y. "Jewish Pirates," 2010 (PDF file on the internet)

8. De la Bandera, Juan, **Relaccion de la Florida,** 1568. The chronicles of the Juan Pardo expedition.

9. Ibid.

10. Hakluyt, Richard, **The Principall Navigations Voiages and Discoveries of the English Nation** (Imprinted at London, 1589) Volume 9, "The Deposition of Nicholas Burgiognon."

11. Gatschet, Albert S., **Migration Legend of the Creek Indians,** Vol. I, Philadelphia: D. G. Brinton, 1884.

12. Capponi, Niccolò, **Victory of the West: The Great Christian-Muslim Clash at the Battle of Lepanto,** Da Capo Press, 2006.

13. http://en.wikipedia.org/wiki/Iberian_Union.

14. White, Robert W., **A Witness For Eleanor Dare,** Long Beach, CA: Lexikos., 1992.

15. Presnell, Lowell, **Mines and Minerals of Western North Carolina,** Alexander, NC: WorldCom, 1999; p. 13.

16. White, Robert W., Ibid.

17. http://www.georgiaencyclopedia.org/articles/history-archaeology/spanish-exploration

18. http://en.wikipedia.org/wiki/History_of_Armenia

19. Alexandre Herculano, *História da Origem e Estabelecimento da Inquisição em Portugal* (English: History of the Origin and Establishement of the Inquisition in Portugal, translation of 1926).

20. Duncan-Hart, Ron, **World Politics, Illegal Jews, and the Inquisition of Cartagena,** Society For Crypto Judaic Studies.

21. Thornton, Richard L. "North Carolina rock's inscription will ultimately change history," The Examiner, December 12, 2010.

22. Rochefort, Charles, **History of the Caribby-Islands** (1665 in French, 1666 in English) Chapter 8, "Paysage au Apalache" p. 241. French Huguenot survivors were allowed to remain in the capital of Apalache and converted the king to Christianity.

23. http://www.georgiaencyclopedia.org/articles/history-archaeology/spanish-exploration

24. "Ruiz de Salazar Vallecilla, Royal Governor of Florida", Spanish Pathways in Florida, 1492-1992.

25. Ibid.

26. http://www.encyclopediavirginia.org/Bland_Edward_bap_1614-1652

27. Roth, Cecil, **A Life of Manasseh Ben Israel, Rabbi, Printer, and Diplomat,** Philadelphia: The Jewish Publication Society of America, 1934.

28. Rochefort, Charles, Ibid.

29. Salley, Alexander S. J., **Narratives of Early Carolina,** New York: Charles Scribner Sons, 1911: p. 27.

30. Talbot, Sir William (Governor of Maryland) **The Discoveries of John Lederer, In three several Marches from Virginia, To the West of Carolina, And other parts of the Continent: Begun in March 1669, and ended in September 1670.**

31. Summers, Lewis Preston, **The Expedition of Batts and Fallon: A Journey from Virginia to beyond the Appalachian Mountains, September, 1671.** From Annals of Southwest Virginia, 1769-1800; 1929.

32. Thwaites, Reuben G., **Father Marquette** New York: D. Appleton & Company, 1902.

33. Woods, Abraham (Virginia Commonwealth Archives) **Letter from Abraham Woods to John Richards concerning the Expedition of James Needham and Gabriel Arthur in 1673 and 1674 from Petersburg, VA – August 22, 1674.**

34. Eric E. Bowne, **The Westo Indians: Slave Traders of the Early Colonial South,** Tuscaloosa, AL: University of Alabama Press. pp. 121–123.

35. Redding, Katherine (Translator) **Plans for the Colonization and Defense of Apalache, 1675.** University of Kansas: General Archives of the Indies, Seville. (Audiencia of Santo Domingo 58-2-5) Florida June 15, 1675.

36. The South Carolina Encyclopedia, p. 1015.

37. Shepherd, Murial Early, **Cabins in the Laurel,** Chapel Hill: University of North Carolina Press, pp. 13-14.

38. Webber, Mabel (January 1936). "The First Governor Moore and his Children". *The South Carolina Historical and Genealogical Magazine* (Volume 37, No. 1).

39. Kennedy, N. Brent, **Melungeons-America's greatest cultural mystery,** 2002.

40. South Carolina Department of Archives and History; Records in the British Public Record Office relating to South Carolina, 1663-1782.

41. Kennedy, N. Brent, **The Melungeons: The Resurrection of a Proud People,** Macon: Mercer University Press, 1997; pp. 115-116.

42. Caldwell, Joseph, "Trends and Traditions in the Prehistory of the Eastern United States," American Anthropological Association, Memoir No. 88, 1958.

43. Lawson, John, **A New Voyage to Carolina,** London, 1709.

44. http://www.chattoogariver.org/?page_id=1635

45. Thornton, Richard, "Stone inscription proves early presence of Jewish settlers in the Appalachians," The Examiner, April 15, 2011.

46. Ramsey, William L., **The Yamasee War: A Study of Culture, Economy, and Conflict in the Colonial South,** University of Nebraska Press. 2008.

47. South Carolina Department of Archives and History; Records in the British Public Record Office relating to

South Carolina, 1663-1782.

48. Kennedy, N. Brent, **The Melungeons: The Resurrection of a Proud People**, Macon: Mercer University Press, 1997

49. Ibid.

50. James Adair, **The History of the American Indians, particularly those Nations adjoining the Mississippi, East and West Florida, South Carolina**, London: Edward & Charles Dilly Printers, 1775.

51. Richard Thornton owned and restored Col. John Tipton's home in Shenandoah County, VA.

52. Owsley, Harriet Chappell, **John Sevier Papers (1752-1815)**, Nashville: Tennessee State Library and Archives.

53. Jones, Charles C., **Antiquities of the Southern Indians, Particularly of the Georgia Tribes**, Tuscaloosa: University of Alabama Press (Reprint) 1873, 1999: p.48.

54. Presnell, Lowell, **Mines and Minerals of Western North Carolina**; p.13.

55. Richard Thornton was Principal Planner and Historic Preservation Planner for Cobb County, GA at the time.

56. http://www.historical-melungeons.com/ac1899.html

CHAPTER THREE

El Infierno
Nodoroc: Hell

FOREST NEAR NODOROC

Photo of Nodoroc today by Bettie Godfrey

" Going a little nearer it was found that not a sprig of vegetation
of any kind grew near it and that the timber growing in the vicinity was
badly dwarfed."

Nodoroc-Hell

This chapter consists of excerpts from The Early History of Jackson County, having to do with the twin mysteries of The Wog and Nodoroc. These excerpts will be followed by a discussion of names which appear in the narrative. For the few spelling mistakes in the original which interfere with meaning we have add [*sic*—MR] so that corrections can be distinguished from those of the original editor.

Excerpts from

The Early History of Jackson County, Georgia

Animals Together With Some Incidents Relating to Them—The Mysterious Wog

Though the species of animals found in the primeval forests of this country by our ancestors, were not so many as those living in the jungles of Africa or in the plains of Asia, yet they were quite numerous. Some were dangerous and other harmless. At least one distinguishing characteristic applied to every one of whatever kind—all were sleek and fat—none were poor or lean. All were wild, but some were more gentle than others. As everywhere else the vicious animals were not the wildest. Nothing approaching a domesticated animal had ever been seen by a native of the country except two horses of which they were much afraid at first, thinking that the horse and his rider were one and the same creature.

While the wolves, panthers and bears gave the first white settlers of this part of the country much trouble, still another animal whose existence has often been disputed, inspired those who professed to have seen him, with more fear than all the others combined. It was the Wog, not Woog as it has sometimes been called. Many of the people who first lived at and for several miles around old Jug Tavern from its first settlement to about 1809, claimed to have seen him at their houses. As the character of the people who first lived there will be shown as this narrative progresses, the reader will be at as much loss to know how he can afford to dispute their word as he is to believe what they have said. At any rate the writer tells the story as it was told to him; but, perhaps, with a little more evidence than any reader has.

The wog is said to be a jet-black, long-haired animal about the size of a small horse, but his legs were much shorter, the front ones being some twelve inches longer than the hind ones. This gave him something of the appearance of a huge dog "sitting on its tail," and when walking seemed to require him to carry forward one side at a time. His tail was very large, all the way of the same size, and at the end of it there was a bunch of entirely white hair at least eight inches long and larger in diameter than the tail itself. Whether sitting, standing or walking this curious appendage was in constant motion from side to side, not as a dog wags his tail, but with a quick upward curve which brought it down with a whizzing sound that could be distinctly heard at least when twenty-five or thirty steps distant. But the most distinguishing feature of this horrid tail was that it revealed the presence of the monster in the dark—the only time he ventured to go abroad. His great red eyes were very repulsive, but not so much as his forked tongue, the prongs of which were thought to be eight inches long and sometimes played in and out his mouth like those of a mad snake. Really the meanest feature about the beast was that his bear-like head contained a set of great white teeth over which his ugly lips never closed.

The Indians told the first white emigrants that so long as the wog was left undisturbed he would not molest anyone—that he would sometimes visit their houses—go around them—if a light were inside, poke his tongue through any opening he could find between the logs, and then go away. Pioneers were not only quick to learn this lesson, but also carefully followed the instruction.

During the years formerly mentioned, the wog made several visits to houses in the territory to which reference has been made. Those inside the house, though they had not seen the flirting of his white plume, knew of his presence by its whizzing sound, by the poke of his horrid tongue through the cracks of the wall, and notably by the mortal fear with which he inspired other creatures outside. Dogs and cats ran away and in some instances were scared to death. Horses snorted, cattle moaned and chickens flew from their roosts in all directions.

Thus having seemingly accomplished his only mission—to frighten everything out of its wits—he gave a loud snort and still twirling his white signal from side to side, went ambling away, and welcome was the going.

The foregoing is, in substance, the description given by Alonzo Draper who lived and died in the territory of the wog, and also by Thomas C. Barron who died near Apply Valley in the '40's of the last century.

Let me repeat: I give the account of the wog as it was given to me. It is hard to confess that one believes that there was such a thing and one hates to say that he does not believe the word of these old citizens. The writer must leave the matter to you, dear reader.

THE WOG

What the Wog May Have Really Looked Like

Pet Wog owned by co-author, Richard Thornton, going for leisurely stroll behind his mountain cabin.

"As I have already said, Nodoroc is hell, and the wog that passed through
Snodon not long ago, is the devil and makes his headquarters there, where no
one who gets in ever gets out."

A short time after the chief's visit the country was thrown into confusion by the always dreaded visit of the "WOG." Though his appearance seemed to be familiar to some of the natives in the surrounding country, none of the white people had ever seen him.

It was a few hours in the night. The half moon hung low, and barely gave light enough to reveal the outlines of an object; just enough to make shadows that swayed back and forth in the passing breeze seem ghostly. As usual there were sentinels in the timbered circle; for now that friendship of the natives was doubted, the white people, though few in number, managed to know almost everything that was carried on in the country. Looking to the four points of the compass stood the Draper family and Abe Trent, all heavily armed, Helen's position facing to the east. At her feet, curled up nearly into a ball, was Lion, a huge Egyptian dog as fierce and almost as powerful as a mad tiger. Suddenly the dog unrolled himself. "TOO HOO" broke the reigning silence. It was Helen's signal to the other sentinels that something unusual was on hand. Lion's growl always meant something.

The girl stood looking and listening. Lion was at her side, bristles erect and occasionally giving a low growl; lower than before. Like an apparition emerging from the ground Abe Trent appeared on the other side. She realized that she stood between two powerful friends. Just then her father and mother came near, and Mrs. Draper, pointing across the field whispered, "LOOK." Lion increased his growls, and all plainly saw a wolf enter the field for a short distance, look around, and then hastily retreat. Another and another did the same until a dozen or more appeared and looked across the field as if in doubt as to what they should do. While thus looking, they suddenly scampered away and disappeared in the woods.

While wondering at the unusual action of the wolves, a dark object that appeared to be carrying a white flag, emerged from the woods and stopped at the outer rim of the field. It was then seen that the white flag was waved from side to side like one motioning to another to get out of the way. This continued for several minutes when at last the dark object moved forward still flourishing its white banner. When little more than half across the field a whizzing sound was heard as the flag went back and forth like a boy cracking his hickory bark whip. Even Lion became uneasy, and turned his growls into low whines. This was significant to all. While seeing that their guns were in order Mr. Draper hurriedly whispered—

"The good Lord! It's that infernal wog!" As bad as Lion had seemed to be scared, his courage returned and it required all of the family's efforts to keep him from meeting the still advancing monster. Mr. Draper's rifle carried an ounce ball, and though he had heard that it was best to let the creature alone, and that its hide was impervious to a bullet, he felt sure in the light of past experience, that he could, to use his own words, "send a leaden messenger clean through any part of its body, or plug one of its fiery eyes out either." He was, however, persuaded to wait for further developments, and the party retired to the house, barred the doors, and stood by their guns, axes and knives, awaiting the gage of battle, if need be.

The near approach of the animal was plainly indicated by the whiz of his tail, and when he reached the door he made a noise similar to the long-continued hissing of a goose. Having done this several times, he began his serenade around the house and finding a small opening between the logs, he poked his forked tongue through it as if trying to impale somone between its slimy prongs. Lion saw this and rushed to grap [*sic* "grab" MR] the tongue, but Mr. Draper succeeded in stopping him just in the nick of time. Having thus twice gone around the house, he gave a short shout similar to one made by a wild hog in the woods, and going west, slowly disappeared. Awhile after the animal left, a light tap was heard at the door. It was Mera who said that her father had seen the wog going away, and that she had come to see if her friends were safe, and to offer such assistance as she might be able to give. When asked why she was not afraid to be out at such a time, the noble girl modestly replied that she could outrun anything that carried along one side at a time. Though evidently willing to return alone, Abe Trent would not allow her to do so, and shouldering his rifle he accompanied her home "with as much pleasure," he said, "as I ever felt in my life."

It appeared that the Draper family was the only one visited by the monster at Snodon, and that after leaving there he was not heard of until he reached Haitauthuga, a small settlement of wigwams that stood on the plain now covered by the fine oak grove east of the residence of Rev. H.N. Rainey at Mulberry. There lived Siloquot, a head man among the Creeks, and a sort of politician. He was one of the signers of a treaty made at Shoulderbone in 1786, and a man of some consequence. When the unscrupulous wog reached his wigwam there were two Lower Creek dignitaries present, perhaps on official business, and as he began to blow and hiss like a monster goose, they ran to the woods as only scared Indians can run, leaving their host to his fate. But Siloquot found safety in the top of a tall tree where the beast, having hoofs instead of claws, could not follow him.

Though playfully requested, Abe Trent had a real motive for wanting to be absent that evening. He was anxious for an interview with Umausauga in regard to the meaning of the strange word, NODOROC; and feeling sure that his friend had more influence over the Indian than any one else, he desired to transfer the interview to Mr. Strong. The friendship between the two was strong indeed. They addressed each other as "father" and "son," and because of these cordial relations Mr. Strong did not hesitate to comply with his friend's request to conduct the interview. Accordingly after the dance was over Josiah and Abe shouldered their rifles and crosing the river at the shoals, the former remained there to fish, apparently, and the latter proceeded on his mission. He Found Umausauga smoking a corn-cob pipe of which he had become very fond, and seemed to be in excellent humor. "Father," asked Mr. Strong, after some preliminaries, "would it be wrong for you to tell me what Nodoroc means?"

The Indian appeared to be surprised and a little disconcerted; but after thinking a little, asked:

"That what for you want to know?"

Mr. Strong proceeded to tell him the suspicious way in which Talitchlechee had used the word by evidently connecting it with Beadland, and then added:

"Father, when you went around the land with us you showed so many signs of uneasiness that we have never been able to understand. Only a very few natives live on it, and the appearance of Snodon shows that it is in a forsaken country. They seldom pass through it, and seem to be actually afraid of the place. And now, as you well know, that the presence of the white man in this part of the country is beginning to give some dissatisfaction, and inasmuch as you and your brother, Etohautee, together with his son Tata, are already classed with the white people, we must know everything that is going on around us. We have full confidence in the three mentioned, and in the Modin family also, and when any of you want help come to us for it at once. Now, father, what do you have to say?"

"Yes," said the Indian after a long and thoughtful pause, "Talitchlechee fool. He knows Nodoroc nothing has to do with white man. Nodoroc in Beadland is, Umausauga to sell it wanted. White man 'fraid of it not. Indian is—scare him to death. Few have seen it ever. 'Fraid to go. To sell it that is why. Devil lives there. It is hell—Great Spirit not there."

"Please," said Mr. Strong mildly, "talk like Banna and I have taught you to speak, and tell me why you use the words devil and hell when speaking of Nodoroc?"

"Oh, Yes, Yes! I forgot! I'll leave off the old Umausauga and come back to the new man that you and Banna and the grace of God made out of the old one and tell you all important movements of the enemy as they occur, and, of the secret which Indians believe lies hidden in Nodoroc. It is kept a secret only because of the mystery connected with the horrid place.

"As I have already said, Nodoroc is hell, and the wog that passed through Snodon not long ago, is the devil and makes his headquarters there, where no one who gets in ever gets out."

"The Great Scott!" exclaimed Strong excitedly. "I am all anxiety to see the place, and instead of being sorry that it is in Beadland I am glad of it. And now that I know Nodoroc belongs to me and my friends, we will go and see the place very soon. I am sure that all will be glad for you to go with us, show us the way to go, and give us such information as we may need. Will you kindly do so?"

"Yes! Yes! Now that I am not an Indian because I have placed myself on the side of the white man and of the white man's God, and for these reasons have felt myself at liberty to give away a secret in regard to his place of torment, I therefore consent to go. Will Banna go with us?"

"Certainly."

"Then see that she does not go near the horrid, boiling, bubbling smoking place. It burns! It burns!"

No man was ever more mystified than Josiah Strong was by Umausauga's description of Nodoroc. He could not even venture to dispute the Indian's word; yet almost every feature described as [*sic*, "was" MR] so unlike anything he had ever heard of before, that he was lost in wonder and amazement.

"It burns! It burns!" To the party of men and women, who, led by Umausauga, left Fort Strong on the following morning, these words as used on the previous day by their leader, were a profound mystery. The anxious company consisted of Mr. and Mrs. Josiah Strong, Mr. and Mrs. Leon Shore, Helen Draper, Abel Trent, and Edward Belknap. This, with the dogs, left a comparatively strong force at Talasee, which was always well guarded night and day. They went by the way of Calamit, and there they left the Trail and turning to the right, rode through the dense forest to some point on the high plain upon which Chapel Church now stands. There they halted, and looking to the north the leader pointed out a long slender column of smoke which seemed to pierce the region of the clouds. The sun shone brightly and there was not a passing zephyr to break the reigning stillness, while slowly, silently, solemnly, the curling, twisting, airy wreaths of intensely black smoke, marked the exact location of the mysterious Nodoroc, the Indian's place of torment. Doubtless it was the first view of an Anglo-Saxon eye, and very impressive. Said Mr. Strong in an effort to describe the scene:

" I am utterly unable to describe the scene or to express in words the feelings it produces. When I take into consideration the associations connected with it and with the other more awful one described in the word of God I am so overcome with the comparison suggested that I can think only of St. John's words in Revelation—'And the smoke of their torment ascendeth up for ever and ever.' "

The sky above, the air and the woods around, and the faces of all the company, all seemed to be shrouded in a funeral pall. The solemn spell was not broken when the leader again pointed to the column of smoke and all moved forward. Having gone a short distance they entered a valley in which all the animals in the country seemed to have been collected.

Having never seen men and women on horseback before, and perhaps thinking the horses and their riders were one and the same, they scampered off in every direction as if never before so badly scared. Turning slightly from the little valley to the west, the part passed over a narrow plain and descended a gentle slope until they could see the column of smoke forming on the surface of what appeared to be a lake of bluish water. Going a little nearer it was found that not a sprig of vegetation of any kind grew near it and that the timber growing in the vicinity was badly dwarfed. A closer inspection revealed the astonishing fact that the lake was not water, but a body of from three to five acres of smoking, bubbling, bluish mud of about the consistency of molasses, and whose surface ranged from two to three feet below the surrounding solid land. The mud near the banks was slightly in motion, but its action gradually increased towards the center until about half an acre had the appearance of a moderately boiling pot of water. The movement of the smoke which arose from the bubbles was sluggish, and uniting in funnel-shaped form a few feet above the surface, formed the imposing column seen from the distant plain. It was perhaps five feet in diameter at the base, and tapering at the height of at least one-fourth of a mile, spread out like the branches of a tree. Now and then a flickering bluish blaze, like a flame from a smouldering fire, played for a moment over various parts of the boiling area. This made the smoke more dense than when there was no flame, and the boiling was less violent. It was said by those who witnessed this uncommon phenomenon on a dark night, that it produced such horrid feelings as to cause some people to faint and made others so sick that they had to be led away. These emotions were probably produced by the unpleasant stench that arose from the lake when the flames were not flickering over it. The fire fed on the ascending gas that was thrown up by the bubbles and thus destroyed the offensive odor.

There, amid the dismal solitudes of a primeval forest, where the white man never trod before, unknown races of people, antedating the red man, may have stood and wondered over the mysteries of Nodoroc just as did the pioneer company from Talasee; for the column of smoke, the lake of boiling mud, and the flames of fire that played over it must have been indescribably grand and awfully suggestive. Who knows that the place did not mark one of the last vestiges of primeval time when "the earth was without form, and void, and darkness moved on the face of the deep."

It was evident that work of which even the red man knew nothing had been carried on at this curious place during the long gone ages of the past. At the western end of the hot mud lake, and fifty steps from its margin, there was a triangular stone house whose sides were equal, twelve feet long and eight feet high. The stones of which it was built were roughly dressed, but well enough for them to fit closely and remain in place steadily. They were of various dimensions, the largest being heavy enough, perhaps, to require two men to carry them. In the east wall, facing the lake, there was an opening nearly five feet high and thirty-two inches wide, the sides of which were better dressed than any other part of the structure. The stone immediately above this opening or door jutted out from the wall a little more than two feet as if intended for an awning; but a close inspection showed that it had been used for some sort of ceremonial purposes. The upper side and that part of the wall facing it indicated the long-continued action of fire, showing like the more elaborate and artistic altars at Yamacutah or Tumbling Shoals the observance of such sacrificial rites as are attributed to the prehistoric races of the country.

The floor of this equilateral triangle was of the same material as the walls, and in the west corner was a solid, hewn stone altar having three steps, on each of which were the same signs of fire as shown on the projecting stone over the door. Both were probably used in conjunction for the same purpose. In 1837 Gov. George R. Gilmer purchased this altar,* and in the spring of 1900, it was still where Mr. Gilmer placed it in the front yard of his residence in Lexington, Georgia.

The indications were that the triangle had been covered, but no evidence of the material used has survived the rush of the sweeping years that have come and gone since it first began to decay.

The walls were covered with a greenish gray moss which must have been the growth of ages. Seemingly one layer, or the growth of a long series of years, had died, and another had grown upon that, and another and another, until the whole bed was, in some places, from six to eight inches deep. A few badly dwarfed oak and chestnut bushes were growing in the moss, and their roots had forced themselves between the stones.

---

*Quite a number of the stones are still in the yard; but many have been carried away by curio seekers. Dr. W.H. Reynolds occupies the old home at present, 1914—Ed.

All present were of a cheerful disposition, but now as they realized that Umausauga's declaration, "It burns! It burns," was really true; that a dry piece of timber thrown into the boiling mud was instantly burned to ashes; that a heavy rain which had just fallen evaporated as fast as it fell; and that the only effect was to increase the volume of smoke, the entire party became solemn and thoughtful. Even Helen Draper failed to shout, "Hurrah for success," and settled down to serious meditation. When at last roused she turned to Mrs. Shore and said, "My dear Ruth, I am about ready to believe that we have fallen into the hands of Aladdin and his lamp and that we have been transported to the shores of the Dead Sea. Have you seen any apples of Sodom growing about here?" "No, child, no," answered Ruth, with a faint smile, "but talking about apples makes me hungry. What do you all say?"

It was early noon, and having brought an ample supply of provisions with them, all joined in a hearty dinner at some distance from the lake. "What is that?" asked Ruth as she munched a piece of broiled fish and sniffed the air. "The old wog is getting his breath," replied Josiah Strong, " as he always does just at noon. Father Umausauga warned me of this, but I had forgotten to mention it."

A brisk breeze had set in from the southwest, the leaves fluttering, the tree-tops waved back and forth, the column of smoke dissolved, and in whirling eddies went chasing each other over the ground and through the air, and the stench from the lake became almost intolerable. The breeze continued for a short time only, just long enough, the Indians believed, for the monster that inhabited it to get a good breath. It was afterwards found that this strange phenomenon occurred at time of full moon only. When the wind had subsided Umausauga, by request, gave the following account of Nodoroc, repeating a few things that he had formerly mentioned to Mr. Strong:

"To the mind of the Creek Indian Nodoroc means about the same as hell does to the white man, and Wog corresponds to devil, or Satan. For the meaning and application of these names I am indebted to my darling Banna, and I have full faith in all that she says. I was myself once so much afraid of the wog-devil that I sold the land on which he mostly traveled, and only a few of my race will live on it. The Creeks believe that all bad spirits are sent here and when their bodies die and sometimes they die here and the wog smooths over the hole they make when entering the mud by sweeping his ugly tail from side to tide. [*sic* "side" MR]

"When one of you told Talitchlechee that you kept men in a hole and took them out as you needed them, he doubtless thought that Nodoroc was meant; and I am of the opinion that that thought of the old chief had as much to do in calming down his fiery spirit as the mortal dread that he and all his warriors have of your keen cracking rifles.

"A long time ago the place was hotter than it is now. Even when I was a boy you could sometimes see solid sheets of flame shooting over the surface like lightning in a southern storm-cloud; and the boiling mud would pop and crack like a burning canebrake. All this made people, and its present condition still makes people believe, that the wog was mad because enough bad spirits were not sent to him. This belief caused innocent victims to be thrown into the horrid place to satisfy revengeful and overbearing natures and to keep the wog from visiting them at night.

"But all the victims that have suffered here were not innocent. Many years ago a woman who lived at Jasacathor killed and ate one of her own children. A hunting party made the discovery and reported the matter to Urocasca, the head man at the time. Finding the report to be true he ordered her to be thrown head foremost into the hottest part of Nodoroc. The old wog was said to turn over when she struck the mud, and sweeping his tail back and forth over the hole she made, the wretch, though often heard, was never seen again.

"Many dark nights she has run over these hills squalling and screaming like a demon while a troop of children followed close behind her shouting and clapping their hands as if greatly enjoying her misery. Her name was Fenceruga, and since that time it has only been used to scare children.

"All prisoners taken in war and those who are condemned to death for crime are thrown into Nodoroc by men called Honoras. At the battle of Rodoata the Creeks captured nine prisoners. They were brought here and thrown into the boiling mud. It was a difficult matter to find a man who was willing to be an Honora, and though not one myself, I saw the prisoners thrown in just where there was a blue blaze of fire playing around them. They did not seem to care for anything until the flames touched them. Then all gave the Cherokee scream of lament. Owocowah! Owocowah! I did not care for it then, but O it seems so terrible, terrible now.

"I never had a wife though once I dearly loved a beautiful girl, and I love her memory still. She was as dear to me as life itself. Yes! Yes! she was much dearer than my life. Her name was Nere Nara. She lived at Snodon where Modin now lives. She was Nyrulyn's sister; with soft and lovely eyes like those of the red deer. Like the full round moon in all its glory, her face with dimpled chin was no akin to earth and seemed to rise and set with the morning and the evening stars. Glad and musical was her laugh as the water ripples over the rocks at Talasee, and her cheeks were as lovely as dewdrops in the morning sunshine. As Nyrulyn's hair is long and glossy so was Nere Nara's, though a little, just a little, wavy—not so much as Banna's is now. She was as fleet of foot as Mera, and as bright as Mera, too. But Nere Nara is gone, now—gone to live beyond the stars in the Happy Hunting Grounds of her fathers—gone to the white man's Heaven where, Ouska! Chouska! Loak (Glory to God!) I will meet her again sometime—meet my lost Nere Nara beyond the stars! Ouska! Chouska! Loak!

"I was to carry my loved one to Adabor, the wigwam on the hill, at time of the next round moon, but Watleskew, a Choctaw warrior came to Snodon and fell in love with Sunrise—Nere Nara means Sunrise. He talked love to her for a long time. She would not talk love to him. That made him mad. He buried his tomahawk in her head. She died on the very spot where Banna gave herself away to Mr. Strong. Her murderer fled towards the north. I had the winds of a bird to run, and the eye of an eagle to follow his tracks. I ran in front, Etohautee and Notha Neva, her brother whom you know, kept my tracks hot with their own feet. We came up with him at Thomocoggin, [Jefferson]. Three tomahawks were instantly buried in his carrion body, two in his head and one in his heart, which I, with my own hand, tore from his breast and gave to a hungry wolf that was prowling around the place. We brought the carrion body here. We ought to have brought him alive; but the cries of vengeance called for haste and they were met with haste. With Modin to help us we threw the carrion far into the boiling, smoking lake just where dull, bluish flames were reaching out, as if for other victims, like lightning in an angry storm cloud. I gloried in the deed then. I feel differently about it now. That was the only dead body ever thrown into Nodoroc. Other criminals that died away from here, if buried at all, lie on the surrounding hill. Look, you can see many graves. It is the Home of the Accursed.

"We buried Nere Nara just where she died. There my heart is buried with her. There, too, I want my body to be buried at her side. Will any of my white friends who may live longer than I do promise to bury me there?"

The speaker paused, and looked upon those around him imploringly. Instantly all present pledged themselves to comply with his request, and to procure the assistance of every white man and woman in the country if necessary. A faint smile played over his features, he chased the thickly falling tears from his eyes and buried his face in the palms of his ponderous hands. As on former occasions, Banna went and sat at his side. She tenderly chased his massive brow with her hands, and leaning her head upon his shoulder, wept like a stricken child.

By and by he looked up and said: "Excuse me! This is not my weakness, but my strength—my strength to bear all things for Nere Nara. When she came into my life the sunshine turned into gold, the moonbeams into silver, and the stars into pearls of the ocean, the great blue ocean above, where god unfurls his banner and bids us march on to victory beneath it, Ouska! Chouska! Loah! [*sic,* "Loak" MR]

"But," continued the Indian after a long pause, "when Sunrise was taken away all the glories of earth turned black as the smoke of Nodoroc. I could not see the blooming flowers, hear the singing birds or laughing water. As I thought on these things my blood began to boil as the central fires of the white man's hell and of the red man's together. I swore vengeance against the whole Choctaw tribe. I organized a war party of more than two hundred followers. When almost ready to start on my mission of vengeance the wog began to appear occasionally.

"Some of you have seen him with his thrashing tail, his great red eyes, his grinning lips and forked tongue. At first he scared some of the natives to death, and it was reported all over the country that he snatched dead bodies out of their graves and ate them. This made me uneasy about the precious body of my lost Sunrise who had so suddenly and unexpectedly set in gloom to rise no more. To protect her from the abominable creature I built the great rock pillar which you all know as Nere Nara over her grave at Snodon.

"Its foundation is deep in the ground to prevent the beast from scratching under, and its top is high so as to enable men who watched the grave to protect themselves. Every night for many moons I sat on top of that drear pile of rocks to watch for the coming of the monster. But it was a work of love, and therefore pleasant. Some of my friends were always on watch with me, and one of us was always wide-awake. One time only the dreadful thing came in sight; but after scaring Hoochleohoopah, who lived where Modin now lives, away from the country, passed on without doing any other mischief.

"By and by, when the lovely form of Nere Nara had returned to what Banna calls her mother earth, the watch was discontinued; but though the place is black and dreary, I still continue to go there frequently. Sometimes Banna went with me, and sometimes she went alone. It was on one of these lonely visits that she found the lock of hair that grew on Mr. Strong's head.

"Vengeance against the Choctaws still ran swiftly in every drop of my blood; but another bright light, almost too bright for earth, came bounding into my life. I found a little daughter on the battlefield of Arharra. I carried her home and nursed her with my own hands. All too soon she grew to be a lovely woman—more lovely to me than the rising sun—more brilliant to me than the evening star, and has, in turn, nursed me with her own hands. The Great Spirit has placed her in a happy home. There the glorious light of the white man's heaven fell upon her, and there the blood of a crucified Redeemer made her who was always white, still whiter than snow. I once believed all these things about Nodoroc. I do not believe them now. Banna talked [prayed] to the true God for me. Vengeance is all gone now. I leave that to the God she serves— to her God and to my God. Ouska! Chouska! Loah! Soul answers soul that Banna Mar de Vedo Strong is right, and God is true. Umausauga is done!"

The foregoing is a free translation of Umausauga's narrative.

No speaker ever had a mort[sic "more" MR] attentive audience, nor was any ever more sincere in his final conclusions. Having finished his narrative he slowly walked far up the hill, and facing to the east, reclined upon the ground. Lighting his favorite corn-cob pipe he began to smoke and apparently fell into a deep meditation. His companions were walking about in various directions thinking of the horrid scenes connected with the place. Perhaps the fate of Fenceruga and Wetleskaw was most vivid in their minds; but if such instances were only a small part of what one man knew of Nodoroc, what would be the sum total of all the horrors witnessed at that dreadful place?

While the scattered party was silently thinking over the strange customs of savage life and trying to compare it with the light of a Gospel day, Umausauga rose to his feet quickly, and placing his hand over his mouth to denote silence, hastily joined his companions near the triangle.

"Silence! silence!" he said as he seated himself near Mr. and Mrs. Strong. "There is no danger if you don't interfere, and keep a still tongue."

As a matter of habit more than otherwise, every rifle in the company "clicked" at the word of danger, and Mr. Strong asked anxiously: "What have you discovered, father?" "The Honoras are coming," was his answer, as the Indian pointed across the lake to the south and continued: "They have gotten some poor wretch for the old wog. I saw them stop and tie his hands together. There are six Honoras, and I judge from fifteen to twenty warriors. It is not likely that the latter will come any nearer if—"

While the Indian was speaking six large men, dressed in skins and decorated with feathers came in view from the direction indicated. They were leading a medium-sized man whose steps were bold and firm, and looking straight before him, seemed to advance without a tremor. Arriving at the bank the Honoras took hold of him, three on each side, and swinging him back and forth several times, threw him head foremost into the hot caldron of slimy mud. The body quickly disappeared below the surface, but nothing was seen of the wog or of its trowel-like tail by the silent and almost breathless spectators.

With a slow and measured tread, in single file and stooping posture, the Honoras joined their comrades in the distance, and going south, disappeared.

Rendered almost speechless by the dreadful sight just witnessed, the little party was standing in wonder over "man's inhumanity to man" when the silence was broken by the whizzing of a shower of arrows through the tree tops over their heads, and some that struck solid timber fell to the ground near their feet.

"What's that?" asked several at the same time. "I never heard of such a thing before," answered the Indian. "But as they know," he continued thoughtfully, "that white people are here, they shot the arrows to notify you that if you follow them they will shoot again."

"Shoot again indeed!" hissed Abe Trent, through his grinding teeth. "If Josiah and Leon will go with me, we'll quickly show 'em who has the next shot."

The next moment Abe was on his horse and ready for a furious pursuit; but better counsel prevailed; and though thoroughly mad, Abe complied with the wishes of his friends, a common thing for him to do. Helen Draper had not said a word, but was on her horse almost as soon as Abe himself, and with one hand raised to give the necessary signal to send him off at full speed wherever she directed, for by this time Scat was about as well trained as Alborak and Iro.

Having sent out scouts and satisfied themselves that the Indians were gone, Umausauga told the party that he had another message to deliver, and then they would all return home. Every one was at close attention with the first word he spoke.

"Friends, children," he began, "of course I do not know of all the horrors that have been witnessed here. Even those of which I do know something, I have told you only a few. There is one more to which I wish to direct your attention because it relates to Banna, and I have never even told her of it. She was too young to understand it at the time, and I have thought it best not to tell her until now. Though a half Upper Creek, I am not a native of this part of the country. I was born and grew to manhood in Wetumpka [Columbus, Ga.], on the Chattahoochee river. My father, Okokobee, was a ruling chief over the Ufallayak division of the Creek race. My mother, Elota, was a Muscogee woman whose father was also a ruling chief. I am their oldest son, and my sister, Eltomura, is next. When I was about grown my father died. Through the influence of the Muscogees, Nenathemahola was put in my father's place which he filled only a short time. Though entitled to the succession I did not want it, mainly because such a course would have involved my mother's safety. So to shorten the matter I and a young brother, Etohautee, whom you know, came to Snodon where he still lives; but after the passing of several moons I went to Adabor to prepare a home for my lovely Nere Nara.

"Now it is a law of the Creek Nation that when the oldest son of a chief fails to fill the vacancy occasioned by his father's death, that his oldest child shall fill the place, or be put to death, and thus stop the line of inheritance in an unfaithful family.

"Time passed on and by some means unknown to me, Nenathemahola heard that I had a little daughter, and that my friends intended to put her in his place with the title of queen, and make me a Head

Man to lead their warriors in battle and perform such other duties as warriors only are expected to do. This made the chief uneasy, and to get the child out of his way he sent emissaries here to murder her.

"While their plans were being matured Etohautee happened to be in that country, and learning of them, he with nine chosen friends, hastened to give me warning. Again my blood was boiling hot. Just think of it! Murder Banna! Murder my princess whom you all call 'THE BEAUTIFUL!'— whom I call 'THE GOOD!' Dear child! to what danger has she not been exposed?

"Left a little child on the dreary battlefield to perish with hunger and be devoured by wild beasts, left where dead men, growling bears, screaming panthers and howling wolves were her only companions! Next threatened with death if she, a mere child, should not be made a queen, and with death to prevent her from being one. And next, doomed to be carried as a slave to the dismal death-swamps of the south because she refused to become a servant of a villain here. Yes, darling Banna, my tongue can not express the danger to which you have been exposed; but thank God, O thou Great Everywhere, that you are now in the hands of friends who are strong enough and willing enough to protect you from all such dangers.

"Etohautee and our nine friends, together with others who live here remained near me and the little girl until all danger was over. We were careful to keep her well concealed and strongly guarded. We ranged the country over both night and day until one evening about dark four men were seen stealing through the woods near Calamit, while the little girl, then about five years old, was sleeping in the opening beneath the arch of Nere Nara with three men on each side and one sentinel lying flat on top of the pillar. Peacefully, soundly, the child slept there that night; but she dreamed not of the time when she gave herself away at that very place with a promise to become the wife of a stranger of whom she had never heard. This increased our vigilance if possible, for we had learned that all four of the men were very sharp and well calculated to carry on the murderous business in which they were engaged. One of them whom we supposed to be the leader, had the same rare faculty that Etohautee has of going to and from a place while you are watching it without being seen.

"They do this by sliding on the ground just like a snake, and to discover one you must watch for a snake. This is not only a rare faculty, but to him who uses it, is the most advantageous acquirement known to the Indian race. Where one or more is known at all, he is called 'a sythyr' or crawler. Etohautee and his son, Tata, are the only sythrys [sic "sythyrs" MR] in this part of the country, though all of them are very careful to keep this gift a profound secret, which enables them to be still more useful to themselves and their friends. You may now understand how Tata and his father can appear before you at night as if they had come out of the ground at your feet, and be thankful that they are your friends. Perhaps I should not have told you of the sythyrs; but I have done so as a friend, and you will not give me away.

"It is something of a wonder that the crawler leader did not give us more trouble, and doubtless would have done so if we had not had a crawler ourselves.

"One dark, moonless night when I and most of my men were at or near Adabor it so happened that the sythyrs of both parties passed near each other. Fortunately the stranger did not discover my brother who, after waiting a little, turned and followed him to the large rock a few steps above the shoals. There he was soon joined by three others, and there, after a hard struggle to take them alive, all four were captured and securely bound. They proved to be the men who were sent to murder my darling little Banna. That was enough! Just at sunrise on the following morning the four men were hurled, full length, into the boiling mud of Nodoroc."

The speaker paused for breath to give more force to the vehement words that began to snap from his quivering lips. Pointing his long, bony finger towards the smoke he continued fiercely:

"See! See! Yonder, where the blue blazes are chasing each other for a moment, then instantly disappear and come again and again in quick succession, is where we threw them. And Umausauga was avenged in part. Nenathemahola was my mother's brother—a full Muscogee. Hence the influence of that tribe to place him in authority; but it did not do him much good. A few moons after his four emissaries disappeared, he also failed to report, and Banna was beyond his reach. In a council of head men called for the purpose, I transferred all my claims to Eltomura. I am to act as her head man in time of war. Since Banna is now in other hands than mine, I hold myself in readiness to fly to her assistance when necessary. Again Umausauga is done."

The day was now far spent, and two and two in solemn procession, the party hastened to Talasee. Pages of unwritten history had been read that day, and the illustrations were so vivid that every feature was deeply engraven on the minds of all. A ghostly night followed and through its darkness restless sleep and fitful dreams alternate while now and then flickering blazes of fire played hide and seek over the walls.

As the forgoing description of the Red Man's place of torment is the only leading feature of this narrative whose history can be continued, we venture to leave early life long enough to give an outline account of the curious place up to the present time.

That Nodoroc was a mud volcano like those that still exist in various parts of the world, particularly in British Burma, there is no doubt in the minds of those who are familiar with its history of little more than one hundred years ago, and with the history of similar volcanoes which still contain boiling mud from which issue flames of fire and smoke.

The writer knows nothing of the legends connected with the place. He gives them as they were given to him.

Even to this day Nodoroc is a curiosity. It is situated three and one-half miles east of Winder on the plantation of John L. Harris, a substantial citizen of the progressive city. We have heard something of its history for nearly two generations before the country was first settled by whites; have seen its condition when visited by highly intelligent parties in 1794, and will now give a brief outline of its history from the visit of Umausauga and his party to the present day.

For many years after but little attention was given the volcano. In fact, the Indians kept away from Beadland, except when on their war expeditions; and the whites were too busy with clearing the forest and fighting the red man to trouble with such things.

Mr. John Gossett lived nearest the mudhole, as it was called. He cleared a large field that almost surrounded Nodoroc. One morning when he and his good wife were in the field they noticed an unusual amount of fog (or what they supposed was fog) hanging over the swamp. As the sun rose higher in the heavens they noticed it did not dispel the supposed mist. But on the other hand the "fog" grew denser, until about 9 o'clock Mrs. Gossett saw a great volume of smoke burst forth from the swamp. She called her husband, who was plowing, to look. Both heard a loud rumbling noise, somewhat like that of distant thunder. Mr. Gossett's horse was frightened and tried to run, so loud was the noise. All at once, the whole surface of the mudhole seemed to rise up into the air. The elements seemed to be filled with hot mud.

It appeared to rise so high and the air was so full of the small particles that it darkened the sun for a few moments. Then came the hot stuff back to the earth, falling all around Gossett and his wife, some striking them bespattering their clothing but doing them no damage, as the little particles of mud were too small.

After this eruption old Nodoroc seemed to settle down several feet and to cool off. In a few years it was perfectly cold and was known the country round as one of the worst "cow mires."

Then the seeds of vegetation began to find their way to the rich mud. A stunted growth was covering the whole surface, though it was quite dangerous to venture on to it. A number of years later it was estimated that more cattle had been lost in the swamp during that period than was ever in the settlement at any one time. This led to the necessity of fencing the swamp which was continued until the coming of the stock law.

Finally, old Nodoroc became the property of John L. Harris, who, always calm and calculating, determined to turn the old time horror into practical use. Accordingly, by dint of much hard work, skill, and a determination to succeed, he drained it sufficiently well to allow cultivation with a hoe. It produced first-class corn which Mr. Harris was careful to carry to solid ground in baskets. In the summer of the second year after the swamp was drained, the writer walked through the growing corn when it was from ten to twelve feet high, and the tops shook to the tread of his feet as far as the corn could be seen.

The ditches were "planked" on all sides with stays between, to keep the soft mud in place, and it was curious to see pure, clear water running along them, as in comparatively recent times no water at all was running there.

Mr. Harris continued to work his newly drained swamp with the hoe for several crops, but of recent years has been cultivating it with horse and plow, and always with highly satisfactory results.

Bones and horns of animals, doubtless those that last disappeared, are ploughed up occasionally.

The whole area, consisting of about five acres, is now in a high state of cultivation, but the surface has been gradually sinking since it was first drained.

Note: Old "Nodoroc" is still owned by Mr. John L. Harris. The Editor visited the place both in 1913 and 1914. The soil is a blue-black in color, very porous and is about four to five feet deep, that is the hard sand pan that has formed is the depth below the surface. In looking down at the "bottom," from the surrounding hills, which are not high, it has the appearance of five acres of land covered with coal dust. Nodoroc is about one-half mile east of Chapel Church and one-fourth mile south of the S.A.L.R.R. on the head waters of Barber's Creek.—Ed.

This ends the excerpts from **The Early History of Jackson County** concerning Nodoroc. What follows is a discussion of the possible origins of some of the names found in that text, as well as how the appearance of Hebrew and other seemingly unusual words in Native languages was interpreted in the colonial period.

In the seventeenth and eighteenth centuries, one of the ideas that held the most fascination for colonists and Europeans concerning Native Americans was the idea that they were descendants of one of the Lost Tribes of Israel, dispersed some two thousand years earlier. In 1650, Amsterdam's chief Rabbi, Menashe Ben Israel, wrote a book, *Mikveh Yisrael* (Hope of Israel), in which he told of a Jewish Dutch explorer in the Americas who encountered Native Americans who spoke words of Hebrew. Other books followed, including, in 1651, *Jewes in America,* by Thomas Thorowgood, and the idea took hold among thinkers such as Cotton Mather and William Penn.

In 1775, James Adair, who married a Native woman, wrote *The History of the American Indians, Containing and Account of their Origin, Language, Manners, Religion and Civil Customs,* noting what he thought of as markedly Jewish customs and vocabulary among Native Americans with whom he came into contact. He wrote that he believed "all the Indians of America to be descended from Jews: the same laws, usages; rites and ceremonies, the same sacrifices, priests, prophets, fasts and festivals, almost the same religion, and that they all spoke Hebrew." [1] Again, all roads of thought led to the Lost Tribes of Israel.

These books reflected, in part, a great interest in biblical history and the Middle East ignited by tales from explorers around the globe. Many scholars extended their range and found similarities between Native cultures in the Americas and Turkish and Arabic cultures. In 1729, Gregorio García in Madrid wrote that many words in Cuzco had Turkish origins, and that *capafi*, the name for a chief in Apalache, had its roots in the Turkish words, *Capi* or *Capit*, of the same meaning.

These ideas fired the imagination, but were born of hopes mixed with inadequate information. What Rabbi Menashe Ben Israel and James Adair did not take into account was that after the expulsion of the Jews from Spain and Portugal, many Sephardic Jews had made their way to this country, some by way of the Dutch West Indies Company which, with the help of wealthy Sephardic merchants, established colonies in Brazil. When the Inquisition spread to Brazil, many Jews fled to the new American colonies and some intermarried with Native populations. Sephardic Jews also arrived in the form of conquistadores, who may have converted to Catholicism but kept their faith a secret. Arabic influence had been great in Spain and Portugal because of the moors, and many Arabic words peppered the languages of Iberia. In addition, the moors, called *moriscos*, who were at first allowed to remain in Spain, were, in 1501, forced to either convert to Catholicism or leave the country. Some made their way to this country as *conversos*, but still kept their faith. Many of those who chose to leave Spain eventually arrived by way of Argentina, and other South American countries. Turks, also, played a part, and many may have escaped shipwrecks along the Florida coast, and left behind their lives as galley slaves to begin anew. James Adair need not have looked so far into the past to make sense of Hebraic words and customs among Native Americans. But while such ideas may have arisen partially from a desire to see Native Americans as persons having a dignity of their own, rather than as backwards savages, it showed that to do so, known and respected ancient cultures had to be superimposed upon them. The truth of who the Native Americans were, especially in the Southeast, is much more complex, and reveals a much more immediate and deeper humanity than could ever be found through a link to an ancient past.

If we start with the assumption, then, that there were many ethnic groups present in the very early colonial days, we can follow the traces that appeared in their language and learn, through those words, a little more about their past. We need not do a detailed linguistic analysis of the kind used to trace a language back to its ancient origins; but rather, an analysis based on sound and kinship to other known languages. And here, it is important to keep all possibilities open—to entertain the idea that a name or word could be Spanish, Portuguese, Arabic, Dutch, French, Hebrew or Turkish, as well as any Native language. Knowing something about how languages change over time helps—knowing that some sounds, like "v" and "b" may have been interchangeable, and that "d" and "t" may be similarly related. Also, it's important to know how Jewish names were changed in Portugal and Spain, and subsequently in Amsterdam, where many Sephardic Jews found refuge.

None of the explanations for the names below are written in stone. For many of them, we can only present possibilities, often several, and let the reader consider what those possibilities mean in the context of history.

Adabor: A town
> *Adab* is an Arabic word meaning to gather to a banquet. The Adab is a collection of rules of good behavior, of hospitality, sacred duty in Islam, and manners. The Adab is also known as "The Path."

Adra Axter, (known as Mino)long lost brother of Nyrulyn, Nere Nara and Notha Neva. He was stolen by the Cherokee when young.
> Although not part of our selected narrative, we've included the name because he is Nere Nara's brother.

> *Adra* is an Arabic word, the name of a town in Southern Syria.

Aakster is a Dutch surname meaning "magpie," which derives from the Old Dutch word, *Ekster*.

Alborak: A young woman's horse .
   Borak or *Buraq* is an Arabic word meaning "lightning." "Al" is a prefix which, like "el", means "the." *Al-Buraq* (still meaning "lightning"), was a mythological steed who came down from the heavens and carried the Prophet Muhammed from Mecca to Jerusalem and back.

   This is one of the most interesting names in the book. For many person's names, we can never know whether or not the people involved knew the original meaning of their name, since generations may have passed since the language from which it came was spoken among them. But *Alborak*, "lightning," is such an appropriate name for a horse, one that would be given today, that it seems almost impossible that the word itself was not understood. The horse belonged to Ruth, a white woman, but was named by an Indian.

   Interestingly, the term *Alboraycos*, was a term used to refer to baptised Jews, who had converted in name only, because they were neither Christian nor Jewish, like Mohammed's Alborak, the mystical steed that was neither horse nor mule. This also points to a possible Sephardic Jewish source, rather than just Arabic. The Arabic influence in Spain through the Moors left many vocabulary words behind in Portuguese and Spanish.

Arharra: The battlefield where Umausauga found Banna.
   Al-Harrah was the site of a famous battle near Medina, in present-day Saudi Arabia. In Arabic, *harra* means "rough, rocky terrain." *Al* means "the," and may at times sound like "ar."

Banna: Umausauga's adopted daughter found after a battle.
   Banah is an Arabic girl's name, possibly meaning *eternity*.

   Since "b" and "v" can change places over time, or be pronounced the same, it's possible that "Banna" was "Vanna," god's gift in Hebrew.

Calamit: Place by a tree – Unrecognizable as a Creek word.

Elota: Mother of Umausauga, a Muscogee woman, daughter of a chief.
   The word *Elota* comes from a Náhuatl word *Elote* or *Elotl* meaning "young ear of corn."
   Elota is a place in Sinaloa, Mexico.

Eltomura: Sister of Umausauga
   In Spanish and Portuguese, *Alto muro* means high wall.
   It's also possible the *mura* is a form of "moor."

   It could also be derived from the Spanish Sephardic name, *Altamiro*, for a town in Spain, Altamira.

Etohautee: younger brother of Umausauga – from Itsate Creek, *Etvwa-te*, meaning "Etowah

People."

Fenceruga: A woman who killed her child

In Portuguese and Spanish *vencer* means to defeat or overcome.
Vincerugo is an Italian surname.

It's important to remember that these names are not fictional, and therefore not necessarily meant to portray characteristics, so it's possible that this murderous woman could have had a name with a positive meaning, such as "to overcome."

Haitauthuga: A small settlement – from Creek, *Hvtvltvke*, meaning "Wind Clan People."

Honora: Warriors whose job it was to throw prisoners into Nodoroc
Honora may come from the Spanish and Portuguese word for honor, *honor*.

Iro: Another horse.
This most likely means "hero," whether taken from the English, or from the Spanish *héroe*. Also possible, the Portuguese word for hero, *herói*. In both Spanish and Portuguese, the "h" is silent.

Jasacathor: A place – Most likely a European or Middle Eastern word.

Lapsidali: A woman who tried to make trouble between the Creeks and the Cherokee
Lapsi is a dish in India made with cracked wheat, sugar, milk and spices. The cracked wheat is also called *Dalia*.
The dish is sometimes called *Lapsi-Dalia*.

Since the Dutch and the Portuguese were vying for the spice trade, the name, if it is correct, could have come from either quarter.

Lapsi means child in Finnish.

Mera: A woman who is described as "fleet of foot," and "bright."
Meira means "giving light" in Hebrew.

In Arabic, it means "princess" or "important woman," and is a variation of *Almera* or *Almira* with the same meaning.

Nenathemahola: Umausauga's uncle, his mother's brother.
This name is a mislitteration of the Creek words, Nene-Tama-Yahola, which mean Path-Tama (tribe)-Speaker. The Yahola is a Creek elected office that means "Speaker of the Town Council."

Nere Nara: Beloved of Umausauga. He said her name meant "Sunrise."
Neri means "burning light" or "my candle" in Hebrew, which seems to carry some sense of a bright sun, and therefore, is a strong possibility.
Narah means "young woman," in Hebrew.

Naaria, also *Naarya* and *Naria,* means "child of God," in Hebrew.

Nodoroc: Site of a mud volcano which the Natives considered the Gateway to Hell.
In Old Dutch, *Noda* means "swamp," and *Roc* means "smoke."

Notha Neva: Nere Nara's brother
Nothus is a Dutch surname. It derives from Darius Nothus II, a high priest of the Jews.

Neva means "speech" in Hebrew.

Nyrulyn*: She was Nere Nara's sister
In Arabic *nurul* means "light" (from *Noor, nur*), and *ain* means "eyes." *Nyrulyn* means "Light of the eyes," or "Shining eyes." *Nurulain* or *Nurulyn,* is an Islamic girl's name.

Nirulen is a name in the Netherlands.

*This name, along with *Notha Neva, Nodoroc* and *Axter,* is clear evidence that there were Dutch Mestizos living in Georgia in the late 1700s and early 1800s.

Okokobee: Umausauga's father, a chief - from Itsate Creek, *Oka-cope,* meaning Water Huge.

Ouska! Chouska! Loak (sometimes "Loah"): Author said that it meant "Glory to God, but these words have a very different meaning.
Oske! Cvske! Loke! means "Drink it! Chop it up! Devour it all!"

Owocowah: Cherokee cry of lament – This word is no longer used by contemporary Cherokees.

Rodoata: A battlefield
Roduarte is a Spanish/Brazilian surname, sometimes written as *RoDuarte*. The "oa" sound would sound like the "ua" in Spanish.

Alternatively, in Arabic *Radhwaa* is the name of a mountain in Medina.

Tata: Umasauga's nephew.
Tata is a Sephardic name, from the Arabic, after the city of Tatta in Morocco.

Talasee: Site of a colony
From Itsate Creek *Tvlase* which means "Off-spring of Tula." Tula was the real name of Teotihuacan in Mexico. The Talasee were located in the Smoky Mountains of North Carolina in the 1500s and 1600s. The name may mean that their ancestors emigrated from the Valley of Mexico.

Talitchlechee: A chief

This is probably from Itsate Creek word, *Tvlase-leche*, meaning, "Lower Talasee."

Watleskew: A Choctaw warrior – unknown meaning, not in the form of a Choctaw word.

Ufallayak : A division of the Creeks
Eufala, an important Creek provincial capital (tribal town.)

Umausauga: An important man – from Creek, *Emale-svke*, meaning, second-in-command – rattle.
This was a war title, meaning that he was a representative of the head warrior.

Urocasca: The head man
It seems logical the *Uro* could be *Oro*, gold both Spanish. In Portuguese. *Ouro*, Portuguese for "gold," is closer in sound.

In Spanish, *casco* means "helmet."

So the word would mean "Golden Helmet," fitting for a head man, a Chief. In Spanish it would have been *casca de oro*.

Note that a helmet would have been gear for a Spanish or Portuguese warrior, but not for a Native American.

Wetumpka: Umausauga's place of birth –
This comes from Creek word, *Oue-tomhkv*, meaning, water fall.
This town was originally located where Columbus, GA is now, at the falls of the Chattahoochee. In the late 1700s, it moved to the confluence of the Coosa and Tallapoosa Rivers in SE Alabama.

Yamacutah: Site of a colony – From Creek word, *Yvmvcuetv*, meaning "to squander, waste money, allow crops to die."

Watleskew: a Choctaw warrior – unknown meaning, not in the form of a Choctaw word.

Wog: The horrible creature associated with Nodoroc.
One possible meaning of Wog comes from the Arabic word *wak* means sullen, morose, ill-tempered; fever or pain.

REFERENCES

1. James Adair, **The History of the American Indians, particularly those Nations adjoining the Mississippi, East and West Florida, South Carolina,** London: Edward & Charles Dilly Printers, 1775.

CHAPTER FOUR

Un Paisaje Cambiado
A Changed Land

NODOROC TODAY

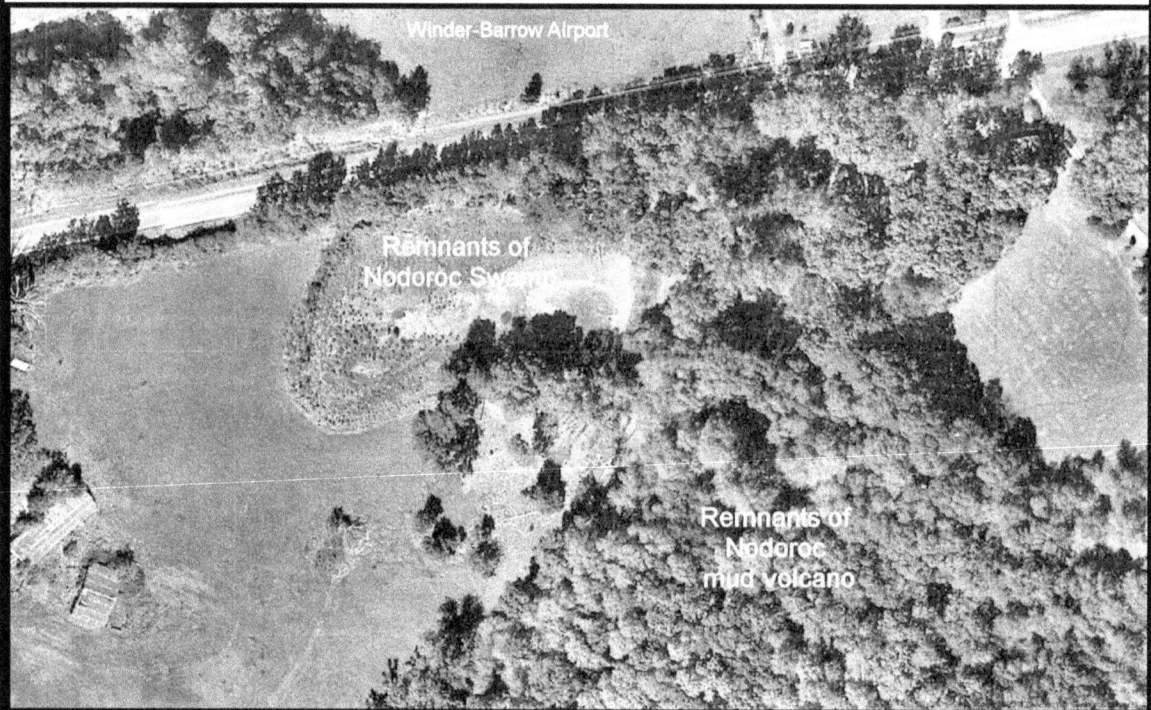

Satellite Image of the Remnants of Nodoroc

A Changed Land

Imagine a scene from a science fiction movie that takes you to the ruins of an ancient civilization on a distant planet. This was the appearance of Nodoroc two centuries ago. A column of black smoke rose from its bowels night and day. A board thrown onto the superheated blue-gray mud would instantly burst into flames. Humans thrown into the inferno would be completely dissolved in a matter of hours by the extreme acidity of the mud. Then one day, Nodoroc exploded and soon afterward became dormant.

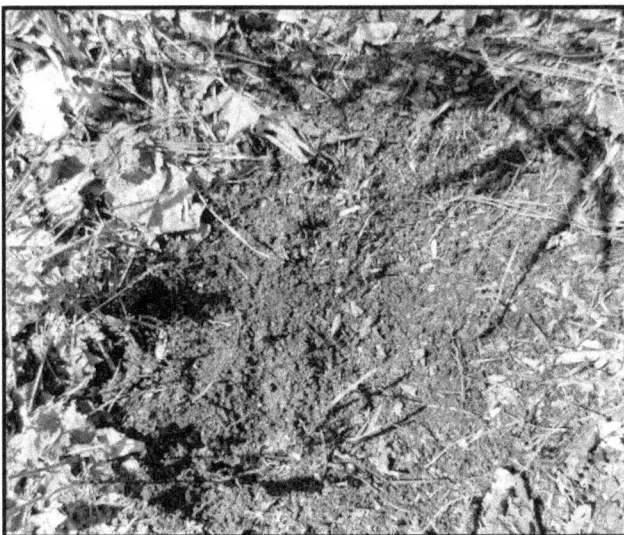

Nodoroc Soil

Today, the Nodoroc site provides little evidence of its violent past. The black top soil around the site has been scooped off and the water table has dropped. It remains one of the most extraordinary geological and architectural mysteries in North America, yet is little known outside Barrow **County.** Based on historical descriptions, geologists have speculatively **classified** it an extinct "mud" volcano, but the presence of extreme heat, flames and smoke suggest that something else was going on before it became dormant.

Without being studied by architects, and long before the existence of the archaeology profession, Nodoroc's sacrificial altar and triangular stone temple were dismantled and reconstructed at the plantation of a Governor George Gilmer, mainly remembered for ordering the arrests of missionaries working among the Cherokees and Creek, and his key role in the Trail of Tears. The stones had been originally quarried and dressed at some time in the ancient past. In the twentieth century, many of the stones were returned to the general vicinity of Nodoroc, but have never been reassembled. One stone is on display at the Barrow County Historical Museum. The only surviving description of Nodoroc from the frontier era is by Georgia author, Gustavus James Nash Wilson.

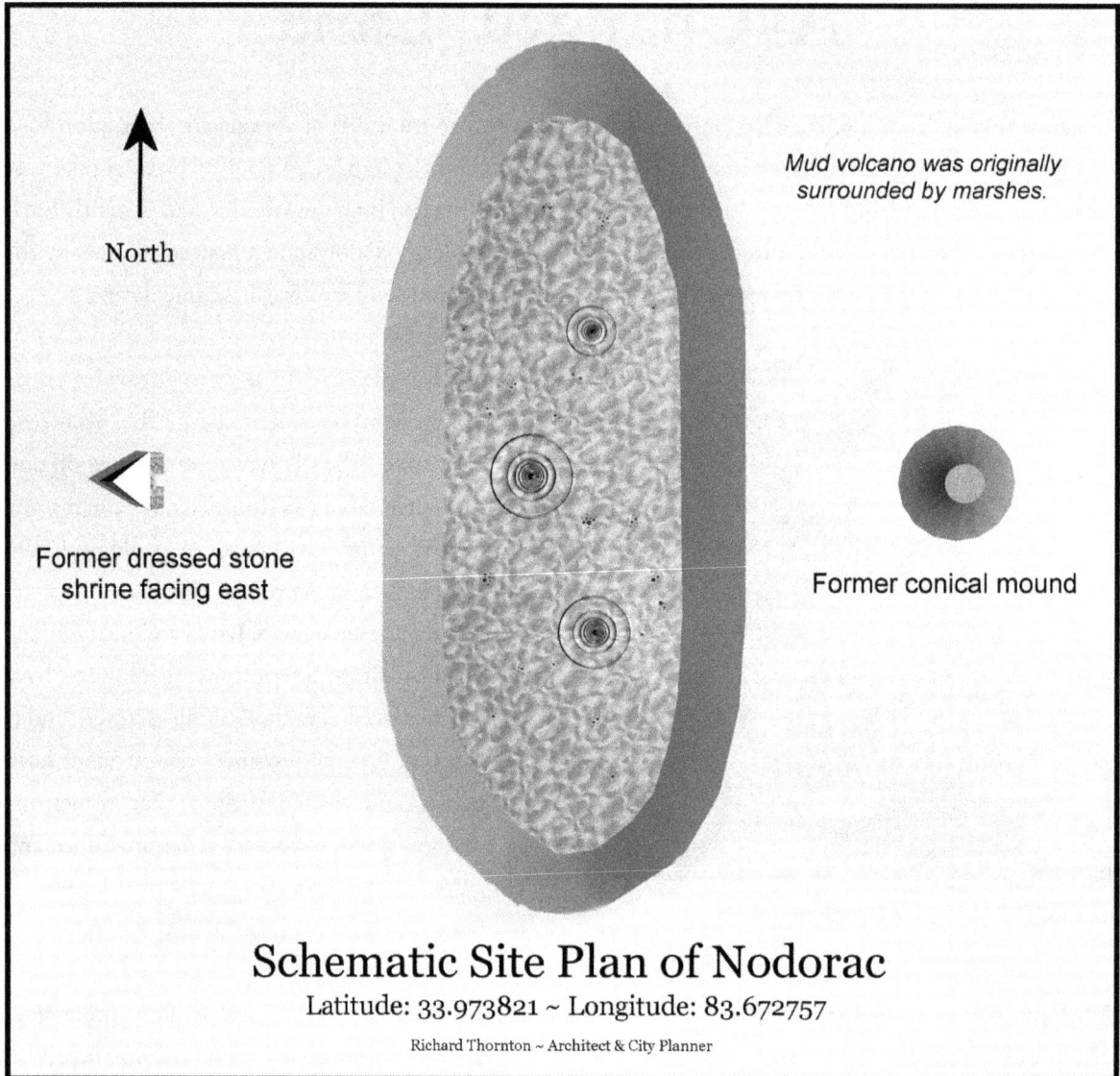

North

Mud volcano was originally
surrounded by marshes.

Former dressed stone
shrine facing east

Former conical mound

Schematic Site Plan of Nodorac
Latitude: 33.973821 ~ Longitude: 83.672757

Richard Thornton ~ Architect & City Planner

Virtual reality image by Richard Thornton, Architect

The name is from what language?

For 250 years Georgia history books have stated that Nodoroc was the Creek Indian word meaning "Gateway to Hell." It is not. No scholar ever looked up those words in a Creek dictionary. The Muskogee-Creek Dictionary tells the reader that the Creek word for "gateway" is *vhvoke* (pronounced ä : hä : kē.) [1] The Creek word for "hell" is *este-nekricv-hute* (pronounced Ĭs : tē – nĭ : klē : chä – hü : tē.) [2] The latter word means "people-burning-building."

Nodoroc is not a Maya or Totonac word, like those of many Creek Indian towns. It is not a Cherokee word. It is not even a French, Spanish, Portuguese or Celtic word.

Nodoroc is literally the combination of two 17th century Dutch (Nederduits) words, *noda* and *rok*. [3] In Nederduits, Nodoroc means "Swamp-smoke." It is a perfect match. The name's origin also means that Georgia's Early Colonial History was VERY different than what schoolchildren are taught.

Northeast Georgia's Pre-European landscape

History textbooks typically describe the Pre-European landscape of eastern North America as a seemingly endless expanse of virgin forests. That possibly may have been true for the northern United States, but certainly was not the case in northeast Georgia.

In 1600, Northeast Georgia had a very different landscape than today. There were vast expanses of prairie artificially maintained by its human inhabitants and grazed by large herds of Woodland bison and white tail deer. The natives intentionally set fire to forest undergrowth and grasslands to keep them clear of shrubs, vines and saplings. Hills would have stood out as islands of giant trees.

The bottomlands of rivers and major creeks were cultivated. Members of the De Soto Expedition, in 1540, stated that while passing through what is now northern Georgia, they never lost sight of cultivated land or houses. [4] By the late 1700s the landscape of the region would have changed radically. The Native American population of the Southeast dropped by at least 90%, during that period. [5] This was due to plagues, European-sponsored slave raids, wars between tribes over deer hunting lands and cultural collapse. [6] The Creeks continued to burn some underbrush until they ceded their lands, but with a tiny fraction of their original population, much of the land would have converted back to forest.

With its plume of acrid smoke rising from scorched, stunted trees, the hundred or so acres that composed the Nodoroc, would have originally stood out for several miles in this open landscape. It was not hidden by dense forests, as was the situation in the late 1700s and early 1800s.

Frontier descriptions of the ruins

About 150 feet from the edge of the west side of the mud volcano were the ruins of a triangular stone temple or shrine, built of dressed stones. [7] Most of the stones were roughly rectangular and about 12-16 inches (30.5 – 40.6 cm) long [7] A large dressed stone formed a lintel over a portal that was roughly three feet (92 cm) wide and five feet (152.4 cm) high. Each side of the shrine was approximately 12 feet (3.67 m) in length. Inside the western apex of the structure was a stone altar with three steps carved into it. The stone structure was situated so that sunlight would illuminate the altar on the sunrise of the Summer Solstice. When viewed by the visiting settlers, there was no roof remaining on the ancient shrine.

Also near the central mud volcano was a conical shaped earthen mound. [8] The Creek Indians living in the vicinity of Nodoroc did not know what was in the mound. They said that it had been built by earlier inhabitants of the region. The Talasee Creek mikko stated that these aboriginals were pagans, who performed human sacrifices at the Nodoroc by throwing victims into the mucky inferno.

Talasee Mikko

Although monotheists, who abhorred human sacrifices to pagan deities, the Creeks did execute particularly heinous criminals and some war captives by throwing them head first into the searing mud. While white settlers and Creek Indians cohabitated the region a woman was executed by such gruesome means. She had killed one of her children and eaten it. Also, during that period a rogue band of Cherokees attacked some outlying Creek-American and Anglo-American farmsteads then committed abominations against some of the women and children. Those invaders, who were not killed outright, were tossed into the inferno.

Europeans first entered the region in 1564. Small parties of Frenchmen from Fort Caroline paddled up the Altamaha River to the Oconee River then took the Lakoda Trail to the vicinity of present day Dahlonega, GA to trade for gold, copper, silver, greenstone and mica that was mined by the Apalache Indians living in the mountains. [9] Captain René de Laundonnière planned to build the capital of New France on the plateau above the head of navigation for large trade canoes on the Oconee. That location is now the University of Georgia. In his memoir, de Laundonnière did not mention Nodoroc.

TALULA-TALWA

Talasee Creek   Muskogee Creek

The words for a modest town in the Creek languages

Virtual reality image by Richard Thornton, Architect

Probable appearance of Talasee, a typical Creek village
in the
Georgia Piedmont during the 1770s

Parties of Spaniards from Santa Elena (South Carolina Coast) continued to trade covertly in the region until around 1587. [10] To date, no mention of Nodoroc has been found in the 16th century French and Spanish archives, but some European trader may have seen it during that period.

British traders from Charleston, South Carolina began traveling along the Lakoda Trail in the 1670s to do business with the Apalache, Kialekee and Kusa Creeks living near Nodoroc. To date, no eyewitness account has been found of a British subject visiting Nodoroc before the American Revolution, but that does not mean that such an event did not occur.

The situation changed immediately after the Revolution. After 1785, only a narrow corridor of Creek Indian land paralleled the Chattahoochee River northward to present day Clarksville, GA. Although part of northeast Georgia remained within the territory of the Creek Indian Confederacy until 1818, local Creek provinces spoke a different language than the Muskogee Creeks, living a hundred miles to the southwest. The locals sold tracts of land to bands of settlers, some of whom had Creek wives. For a period of 20 years, the two peoples generally lived in harmony, then the majority of Creeks moved westward.

While co-occupying the land with Creek Indians, white settlers become aware of the Nodoroc and its fearsome occupants, the Wogs. However, the early settlers had avoided living near Nodoroc because of its acrid fumes and horrific reputation. When the entire region opened up to settlement, it was inevitable that naïve Anglo-Americans would establish farmsteads near the Nodoroc.

Around 1800, settler John Gossett built a cabin near Nodoroc and cleared all the lands around its marshes. Probably, by this time the Wog was extinct or near extinction. Otherwise, it is unlikely that the Gossetts would have settled there. A few years later, perhaps at the same time as the massive 1813 earthquake on the New Madrid Fault, the Gossetts noticed that a dense fog hovered over the Nodoroc and surrounding swamp. Around nine o'clock, the cloud exploded with a rumble and a sharp roar. A great mass of black smoke rose from the Nodoroc and formed a mushroom cloud. After the explosion, the mud barely bubbled and soon became still. The mud dried. Within a few years more, vegetation began creeping into the site. Many cattle still became trapped in the quick sand and died, but the heat, flames, acidity and smoke were gone.

The enigmatic, ancient structures at the Nodoroc

In 1873, historian and amateur archaeologist Charles C. Jones, Jr. wrote that the landscape of the Georgia Mountains and Piedmont was littered with ancient stone structures, when European settlers reached the region in the late 1700s and early 1800s. [11] They consisted of building ruins, terrace walls, stone mounds and effigies. This fact has long been ignored by the region's archaeologists.

Jones was the first to prove that the earthen mounds in the mountains were built by the ancestors of the Creek Indians, not the Cherokees. However, he was uncertain about the stone structures. He speculated that they were built by an ancient civilization that preceded the Creeks. However, by then, many of the stone structures were gone. They had been quickly pilfered by settlers to build foundations and chimneys. Most of the ruins that survived 19th century home builders were crushed in to gravel for mid-20th century highway construction.

Such was the case of the enigmatic triangular stone temple at Nodoroc. [12] Some stones were carried away by settlers until the site was absorbed into the plantation of John A. Harris. In 1837 Harris gave the stone altar to outgoing Governor George Gilmer in gratitude for incessant pressure to dispossess the now-civilized Cherokees and send them on the Trail of Tears. By this time the Nodoroc mud pool was dry, black earth. The altar sat in the front lawn of Gilmer's plantation for many decades. Its current location is unknown, but it probably still exists.

Some stones still were stacked on the site of Nodoroc when "The Early History of Jackson County, GA" was written in 1914. [13] One of the dressed stones had a simple cross formed by two lines on it. This is significant, because an ancient stone quarry has been found in the Chattahoochee National Forest near the Track Rock Gap Archeological Zone.[14] Several of its dressed stones display simple crosses exactly like the one at Nodoroc.

Stacked Stones from Nodoroc
Photo courtesy of Jackson County Historical Society.

The discoverer of this quarry refused to divulge the exact location of his photographs. He is keeping the site confidential to avoid political machinations from local US Forest Service officials like what occurred at Track Rock Gap. [15] He stated that he hopes "that a division of the Federal government more experienced in cultural preservation, such as the National Park Service, will take an active role in protecting and studying the remaining stone ruins in northern Georgia."

Richard Thornton
Architect & City Planner

Richard Thornton
Architect & City Planner

86

In 2002 the National Park Service issued an RFP for a professional study of the surviving stone ruins in northern Georgia, but the contract was never executed because of budget cuts mandated by the invasionof Iraq. [16] By then, though, the Nodoroc triangular temple was nothing but a memory.

The temple or shrine at Nodoroc is the only known example of a triangular, stone structure in the Western Hemisphere. Its architectural form does not appear in either traditional Creek or Maya architecture. In fact, triangular temples are rare throughout the world. The only location where there are a significant number of examples is on the Island of Cyprus in the eastern Mediterranean Sea. Several small, stone, triangular shrines found there have been dated to the Copper Age or Early Bronze Age, roughly 2000 -1600 BC. [17]

Opposite and Above: Temple at Nodoroc
Virtual reality images by Richard Thornton, Architect

Most of the stone structure of the Nodoroc temple has apparently been moved. It did have a quarried stone floor and foundation. Perhaps some of these remain. Even if they are no longer present, it may be possible to locate the temple site with ground radar or kindred non-obtrusive forensic technology. In the past, some amateur archaeologists claimed that the temple was 6,000 years old. This may be true, but there is no proof of the claim and a younger age is likely. However, with no studies by archaeologists or geologists available, it is impossible even to speculate on the temple's age and builders. For now, the Nodoroc must continue to be a mysterious place with many possible interpretations.

Scientific study of the Nodoroc

As Barrow County's population exploded in the late 20th century, the Nodoroc was almost forgotten. Newcomers had no clue about the rich Native American, frontier and geological history of the county. Civic leaders developed a local history museum. Publicity about the Nodoroc attracted the attention of two botany professors from the nearby University of Georgia. [18] They carried out some soil test bores of the original mud pool and wrote a report on its botanical history.

Forest near Nodoroc
Photo by Bettie Godfrey

In contrast, the site continues to be ignored by archaeologists and geologists at the University of Georgia. The terrain of the Nodoroc site obviously contains many fossils and Native American artifacts, but the faculty seems to be unaware of the potential discoveries awaiting them, only minutes from their offices.

The same situation applies to several complexes of stone structures in Jackson County, GA which is immediately north of the University of Georgia campus. The University's historic preservation program has never tried to **track** down and study the surviving stones and altar, which could be of international significance. Georgia Tech's College of Architecture, 40 miles (64 km) away in Atlanta, has also never showed interest in the stone ruins in Barrow and Jackson Counties. As a result, what few facts that are known about Nodoroc, are botanical in nature.

In 1981, paleo-botanists, Dr. Stephen Jackson and Dr. Donald Whitehead of the University of Georgia explored the Nodoroc. They published the report on Nodoroc in 1991 and 1993. Two deep piston cores were analyzed.

The scientists identified two distinct colors in the soil sample cores. The first dated from 30,000 – 26,000 years ago. The other later dated from 4,000 years ago. There were long periods when sediment did not accumulate. The scientists interpreted this finding to mean that the mud volcano has gone through several cycles of violent activity, followed by dormancy. During the long dormant periods, the Nodoroc and surrounding terrain was a marsh, or a cluster of marshes. It is quite possible that it could erupt again in the future.

A mixture of northern and southern tree species occupied the Nodoroc site for much of the past. During the four Ice Ages, the Southern Piedmont was a boundary area between a boreal climate to the north and a sub-tropical climate along the Gulf of Mexico. Like the current boundary area in southern Canada and upstate New York, present day Northeast Georgia was prone to extremely heavy snows when glacially chilled air collided with subtropical air. These swings in climate and weather enabled both hardy species of the northern and southern part of the continent to cohabitate the region.

In 1987, a nature lover named Gary Bolton visited the Nodoroc site. [19] He wrote that tulip tree saplings were struggling to colonize the old pond area. There were "thousands" of crawfish chimneys in the black muck. The substance on the surface was essentially peat, which is a rare phenomenon in the Southeastern Piedmont.

An ancient history of volcanism

The report produced by the two botanists suggests that they were not aware of northern Georgia's volcanic past. Roughly 250 – 300 million years ago, northern Georgia was one of the most active volcanic regions in the world. This was caused by the collision and ultimate separation of the North American and African plates. When the two continents separated, a portion of Africa broke off. It became the Coastal Plain and portions of the Piedmont in the Southeast. In process, mountains were created that were as least as high as the Himalayas, perhaps reached 30,000 feet (9,144 m.) That is why no dinosaur fossils are found in the southern Blue Mountains.

There has never been a comprehensive survey of extinct volcanic mountains in northern Georgia, but the cone shaped structures are concentrated in a diagonal line running roughly west to east. Some of the larger cone shaped peaks are immediately south of the Blue Ridge Mountains in the vicinity of Helen, GA and 42 miles (68 m) due north of Nodoroc. There is also an extinct cluster of volcanic mountains immediately west of Dalton, GA in the northwestern mountains. Apparently, some volcanic activity in northern Georgia is far more recent than is generally assumed. The boulders are still visible on a mountain west of LaFayette, GA. Minor tremblors are common near LaFayette.

In "The Migration Legend of the Creek Indians," the Kashita branch of the Creek Indians, were migrating southward from the Little Tennessee River Valley in present day North Carolina. [20] As they neared a great town built on the side of Brasstown Bald Mountain, GA (*presumably the Track Rock terrace complex,*) they heard a constant rumbling sound from this mountain. They named the mountain, "the mountain that beats the drums."

At times, employees at the Walasi-yi camping supply store on the Appalachian Trail at Neel's Gap, have also occasionally heard drum-like rumbling sounds from nearby mountains. [21] There is a massive collapsed caldera crater immediately adjacent to the Track Rock ruins. These phenomena have not been comprehensively studied by geologists.

The June 20, 1857 edition of the New York Times reported a volcano in Georgia. [22] The article stated that on May 24, 1857 a large hill, 10 miles west of Augusta, GA (known locally as Pigeon Mountain) erupted as a small volcano. For a period of five days, it was the center of numerous earthquakes in the region. It also emitted hot, sulfurous fumes and caused loud explosions. The ground on the large hill became so hot that most of the vegetation and wildlife died.

A possible extinct volcano and adjacent collapsed caldera (also named Pigeon Mountain) is immediately west of Lafayette, GA. It has been the source of minor earthquakes up to 4.5 on the Richter scale, several times in recent years. Pigeon Mountain sits atop an old fault, defined by adjacent Lookout Mountain. [23]

The Wog

One of the strangest aspects of the Nodoroc story mentioned by Gustavus Wilson is the legend of Wog. According to the surviving accounts by white settlers, the Wogs were large animals that primarily ate carrion, but sometimes preyed on rodents, dogs, cats and small livestock when no dead wildlife was available. Wild animals thronged to the marshes around the Nodoroc, but frequently became trapped in their quicksand and quick mud. The Wogs feasted on their carcasses, when the flesh had "properly ripened."

The description of the Wog by white settlers sounds implausible, but was probably based on a real animal that is now extinct. The Wog was said to be the size of a horse, with a head like a lion and stocky rear legs that were 12 inches shorter than the front ones. It had a long forked tongue that was used to probe hiding places of potential meals. Its long black tail constantly wagged horizontally.

Apparently, the Wog was primarily a nocturnal animal. As long as wildlife continued to be trapped in the marshes, the Wogs would satisfy their dietary needs with a bounty of decaying flesh. When the settlers arrived in large numbers, the wildlife population plummeted due to over-hunting and loss of habitat. Hungry Wogs began roaming at night in search of cats, dogs, lambs, goat kids and newborn calves. If none were caught, the Wogs would even dig up human burials that were laid to rest in shallow graves.

The shortage of wildlife also affected the local red wolf population. Normally, the red wolves stayed away from humans, but with starvation they became bold and also began to raid farmsteads. It is possible that many of the livestock losses blamed on the Wogs, were actually the work of wolves. The Wogs DID occasionally come around farmsteads at night though, much to the horror of their occupants. Terrified families would see its long, black, forked tongue probing through cracks in the chinking. For a few years, the carcasses of cattle that became mired in the quick sand and quick mud at Nodorac kept a few Wogs alive, but their days were numbered.

Wogs, Red Wolves and Woodland Bison

Because of the numerous reports of its existence from both Creek Indians and early settlers on the frontier, there is little doubt that a massive carrion-eating creature once lived in northeast Georgia, perhaps in smaller numbers, elsewhere in the Southeast. It was probably a large iguana or monitor lizard like the Komodo Dragon in Indonesia. Both creatures lived primarily off of carrion. A Komodo Dragon will kill live prey, then come back several days later when the flesh has been tenderized by decomposition.

Several major indigenous ethnic groups have a tradition that giant, flesh-eating lizards once stalked the Southeastern United States. These legends were documented by Smithsonian ethnologist, John R. Swanton. [24] The best known legend is that of the *Inzignanin* in South Carolina. The Creek and Cusabo version of the legend described the beast's body length being equal to the height of a man. In addition, this giant, dark-skinned lizard had a tail about five feet long that constantly swung back and forth, just as the Wog was described.

When Georgia was settled by the British in 1733, there were large herds of Woodland Bison roaming the northeastern part of the province and smaller herds elsewhere. As stated earlier in this chapter, Northeast Georgia then contained much open prairieland, created by both the herds of buffalo and by the annual brush fires set by the Creek Indians. The bison congregated at the sites of extinct mud volcanoes. They licked the mineral rich clay. Some of these "buffalo licks" are still visible. The largest and best known is in the community of Philomath in Oglethorpe County, southeast of the Nodoroc. [25] It was visited by botanist William Bartram in 1774. The bison also were attracted to an active mud volcano, the Nodoroc.

The alleged size of the Wog can be explained by the availability of massive bison carcasses. The large packs of red wolves can be explained by the large herds of bison and deer that roamed the prairies of Northeast Georgia.

The Native American deerskin trade and cessation of the annual burning of underbrush almost made the whitetail deer extinct in Georgia by 1800. When European settlers first colonized the Southeast, deer were diurnal herd animals like the bison. At certain times of the year, there might be hundreds of deer in a herd. Their behavior would have been very similar to the antelopes on the African grasslands.

Intense hunting with firearms essentially created a new species of deer that was nocturnal, semi-solitary and a forest browser like goats. Deer with these mutated characteristics were the only survivors of the onslaught.

Bison became almost instantly extinct around 1750 in Georgia when a plague introduced by imported English cattle swept the landscape. [26] Twenty-five years later, when white settlers were first entering the region, the population of Wogs and Red Wolves had probably already collapsed due to lack of bison and deer meat. Cattle trapped in the swampland of Nodoroc enabled a few Wogs to survive, but their time on earth was nearly at an end.

The world of those humans who knew the Nodoroc volcano and the Wog is, indeed, one that is gone with the wind. It is highly unlikely that it will ever return.

REFERENCES AND NOTES

1. Martin, Jack B. & Mauldin, Margaret McKane, **A Dictionary of Creek/Muskogee**, Lincoln: Nebraska, University of Nebraska Press, 2000; p. 243.

2. Ibid., p.251.

3. Van Wely, F. Prick, **Van Goor's Dutch-English Dictionary**, New York: David McKay and Co., 1959.

4. Lawrence Clayton (Editor), Edward C. Moore (Editor), Vernon James Knight Jr. (Editor), Charles Hudson (Contributor), Dr. John E. Worth (Contributor), Eugene Lyon (Contributor), Jeffrey P. Brain (Contributor), et al., **The De Soto Chronicles**, Tuscaloosa: University of Alabama Press, 1996.

5. Denevan, William D., editor, **The Native Population of the Americas in 1492**. Second edition, Madison: University of Wisconsin Press, 1992.

6. Thornton, Russell, "*Native American Demographic and Tribal Survival into the Twenty-first Century*," Indigenous Studies Today, 1 (Fall 2005/Spring 2006).

7. Wilson, Gustavus James Nash, **The Early History of Jackson County, Georgia**, Atlanta: White Printing Co. 1914.

8. Ibid.

9. De Laundonnière, René, *L'histoire notable de la Floride, contenant les trois voyages faits en icelles par des capitaines et pilotes français*, Saint-Germain-en-Laye, France, 1586.

10. Hakluyt, Richard, **The Principall Navigations Voiages and Discoveries of the English Nation** (Imprinted at London, 1589) Volume 9, **Relación de Pedro Morales & Relación de Nicholas Burgiognon.**

11. Jones, Charles C., **Antiquities of the Southern Indians, Particularly of the Georgia Tribes**, Tuscaloosa: University of Alabama Press, 1999 (originally New York: D. Appleton & Co., 1873), xxii.

12. Wilson, Gustavus James Nash, Ibid.

13. Ibid.

14. After the broadcast of the premier of "America Unearthed," a resident of Union County, GA contacted this author via email and phone. He transmitted photos of what appeared to be an ancient stone quarry in the Chattahoochee National Forest, plus several rectangular stones with equilateral crosses inscribed on them.

15. The Track Rock Archaeological Zone in Union County, GA was adopted by rightwing extremists as a political cause. Near the archaeological zone is a training camp for private paramilitary militias.

16. The author submitted a proposal for this project that never happened.

17. http://www.foxnews.com/story/2009/03/27/archaeologist-discovers-cyprus-oldest-religious-site/

18. Jackson, Stephen; and Whitehead, Donald, "Pollen and Macrofossils from Wisconsinian Interstadial Sediments in Northeastern Georgia" Quaternary Research 39 1993.

19. http://www.garymbolton.com/i-visited-hell-in-1987/

20. Gatschet, Albert Samuel, **A Migration Legend of the Creek Indians**, 1884.

21. Personal communication with the author.

22. "A Volcano In Georgia", The New York Times, June 20, 1857.

23. http://sincedutch.wordpress.com/2011/11/14/11132011-georgia-earthquake-near-dormant-volcano-nyt-from-1857-confirms-past-activity/

24. Swanton, John R., **Myths and Tales of the Southeastern Indians**, "The Monster Lizard". Washington City: Smithsonian Institute Press, 1929.

25. http://www.historicoglethorpecounty.com/html/philomath.html

26. Ibid.

CHAPTER FIVE

Los Bohurones

The Bohurons

The Bohurons

This chapter consists of excerpts from *The Early History of Jackson County*, having to do with the Bohurons, a powerful, warlike branch of the Creeks.

An Evaluation of Gustav Wilson's Historical Accuracy

This section of "The Early History of Jackson County" is not in sync with actual historical events in Northeast Georgia during the late 1700s. Cherokees never lived in Jackson, Barrow or Clarke Counties in Northeast Georgia. They had a minimal presence in Georgia between around 1725 until 1785.

The Cherokees lost the 40 year long Creek-Cherokee War catastrophically in 1754. By that time, all of their villages in the northeast tip of Georgia and the Upper Hiwassee River in North Carolina had been burned and abandoned. There was never again a war between the Creek Nation and the Cherokee Nation. In the 1780s and 1790s when the plot of the first chapters of Wilson's book take place, the Creek Nation was at its peak of power. It even built a gunboat navy to patrol the navigable rivers and Gulf Coast. In contrast, the Cherokees were divided and had been forced to relocate most of their villages in northeast Georgia to Alabama because of the Chickamauga War.

After the Cherokee Nation was defeated by the United States in 1777, a renegade band broke off from the main tribe and continued the war against Anglo-American settlers from transient villages in northeast Alabama, southeastern Tennessee and northwest Georgia. Renegade bands of Upper Creeks and Chickasaws joined the renegade Cherokees.

During the American Revolution, a group of partisans, led by Thomas Waters, settled near a small Cherokee hamlet on the Etowah River at the mouth of Long Swamp Creek in Pickens County, GA. This "Cherokee" hamlet probably was not occupied by ethnic Cherokees, because it was a long distance from any other Cherokee village and located in Upper Creek territory. The partisans carried out a reign of terror on the frontier of Wilkes County, which was immediately south of Jackson County.

In 1783, and what was possibly the last battle of the American Revolution, a combined force of South Carolina and Georgia mounted militia under the command of Col. Elijah Clarke and Col. Andrew Pickens attacked the "Cherokee" village. The village quickly surrendered and as a sign of good faith offered a peace treaty written in English, which gave away all **Creek** lands in northeast Georgia, but not any Cherokee lands.

Georgia's government ratified the fraudulent treaty over the protests of the Creek Confederacy. The Creeks in that region had fought as allies of the United States. Neither the leaders of the Cherokees nor the Creeks had signed the treaty. Nevertheless, white settlers poured into the region that included the future Jackson County. In 1785 the Creek Confederacy reluctantly ceded its lands east of the Oconee River, plus, after the University of Georgia was established, a small corridor on the west side of the Oconee, opposite the University.

The Principal Chief of the Talasee Creeks, Hopoithle Mikko, was an ally of the United States during the American Revolution. He lived in what is now Clarke County, GA. He moved to Alabama in 1785. The Talasee Colony was located at the site of the Talasee provincial capital. The Creek Indians continued to own the land between the Oconee and Chattahoochee Rivers until 1818.

After the American Revolution, the Chickamaugas prosecuted a bloody guerilla war against small groups of white settlers, but lost every standing battle fought against militiamen or regular soldiers. There is no record of the Chickamauga Cherokees attacking settlements in northeast Georgia. In fact, most of the non-hostile Cherokees in northeastern Georgia were forced to flee the region because of pre-emptive attacks by units of the Tennessee Militia. Georgia militiamen were not involved.

In 1792, four forts were built in what are now Jackson, Barrow and Clarke Counties because of skirmishes between small bands of Oconee Creeks or Yuchi, and frontiersmen along the lower Oconee River. The bloodshed was on the scale of individual criminal acts by the three ethnic groups, rather than real warfare. The Talasee Creeks on the upper Oconee DID invite white families to settle among them. The unusual gesture was done to protect their villages from preemptive attacks by undisciplined white militia units.

Rumors spread that the entire Creek Nation was about to declare war on the State of Georgia. This caused the panic mentioned in Wilson's book, which drove settlers to seek shelter in the forts. Such a war was averted through diplomacy. The region where the conflicts occurred between the Creeks, Yuchi's and aggressive white settlers was ceded to Georgia. Native families that had good relations with their white neighbors generally remained in the region.

Inaccurate Statements about Native American Culture

It is obvious that Gustavus Wilson's account of Georgia's frontier days was based on second hand oral history from his father's generation rather than eyewitness accounts written down as they happened. He inserted several inaccurate details about Creek Indian culture. He apparently drew these details from reading James Fenimore Cooper novels, because words he used were typical of the Northeastern Woodland Indians. For example, Wilson called the Creek houses, *wigwams*. By the 1780s the Creeks had been living in log houses for at least two generations and been using firearms almost exclusively for three generations. Prior to that era, they lived in thick-walled, multi-room, wattle & daub houses.

The main Creek house was called a *choko*, the Itza Maya word for "warm." Wilson called the lightly built summer house, woven from split cane, a *wikiup*. Its Creek name was *chiki*, the Itza Maya and Totonac word for house. *Chiki* was derived from the Maya word for weaving a basket.

Wilson portrayed the Talasee and Bohurons as autonomous political entities, such as one might have found on the Great Plains in his era. For at least a thousand years the ancestors of the Creek Indians were organized into provinces governed by a capital town, known as an *e'tula-mako* in Itsate Creek or an *etalaw-mikko* in Muskogee-Creek towns. Within a province might be citizens speaking several dialects and languages, but using either Itsate or Mvskoke to communicate with each other.

In the 1700s the provinces were subject to a National Council (*Tvlwa-vike Ennvkvftetv*) composed of all the leaders of all the provinces. Between 1776 and 1824, the Principal Chief (*etvlwamikko*) of the Piedmont Talasee Province was *Hopoithle Mikko*. There was another Talasee Province in southeast Georgia. All of the Talasee had originated in the Great Smoky Mountains.

The tomahawk was never a common weapon used by the Creeks. They carried large knives. For close, hand-to-hand combat they would also use a 32"-36" war club fashioned from the root of a wild cherry tree, studded with sharp blades or an iron spike. A tomahawk would be almost useless against a warrior armed with such a weapon. Just like Anglo-American frontiersmen, their primary weapon was a rifled musket that doubled as a long club, if the gunpowder ran out.

The opening passages of Chapter Five in "The Early History of Jackson County" discuss a bundle of arrows that were supposedly left over from King Phillip's War." King Phillip's War was a major Native

American uprising against the English settlers that occurred between 1676 and 1678. If such a bundle of arrows even existed on the Georgia frontier in the 1780s, they would be badly deteriorated because of the crude adhesive used by New England Native to affix arrow points and feathers. Wilson stated that a wooden arrow shaft was superior to the Creek's arrow cane and that their black flint points came from New England.

Actually, the obsidian-like black chert Wilson described was mined in northern Georgia and northeastern Alabama and exported to other tribes. An arrow-cane arrow shaft was inherently faster and more accurate that a shaft made from a wood sapling. The cultivated arrow-cane was rock hard, perfectly round and perfectly straight. This anecdote is more evidence that Wilson expanded the original frontier stories with second-hand information.

On a few occasions, Wilson described Creek men wearing feathered hair dresses. In general, multi-feathered war bonnets were not a tradition in the Southeast. For at least 900 years prior to the time period of this book, the ancestors of the Creek Indians wore cloth turbans. Creek women of high political status also wore a type of turban. This practice continues among the Mayas today.

Wilson's anecdotes also included some problematic ethnic identities. He places Choctaw men in Georgia during the late 1700s. This was so unlikely as to be considered impossible. The Choctaws and Creeks were enemies throughout much of the 1700s. The Choctaws never lived in Georgia. Some Chickasaws did live in southwest Georgia and the northwestern tip of Georgia. Either Wilson or the original person telling the story arbitrarily chose the label "Choctaw" to mean a traveler from another Native American tribe.

Wilson did not seem to be aware that the "Indians" that he described in his book were for the most part mestizo's . . . people of multi-racial heritage. The authors translated the names of most of the characters and those names were of both Creek origin and several ethnic groups in Europe and the Middle East. The use of personal names from several widespread origins is substantial evidence that non-indigenous peoples had been living among the Creek Indians for a considerable period of time.

The homeland of the Talasee, which was the Little Tennessee River Gorge in the Great Smoky Mountains, is where a rock inscription exists that memorializes a Jewish wedding on September 15, 1615. It is located on the top of Hooper's Bald Mountain in Graham County, NC.

Although there are flaws in the early chapters of Gustav Wilson's manuscript, there are also historical facts within his text that can be collaborated. These chapters can be viewed in the same perspective as the contents of James Mitchner's masterpiece, "*The Source.*" They are actual historical events and people embellished with some fictional personalities and imagined dialogues.

Excerpts from
The Early History of Jackson County, Georgia

Since the rumors of a Cherokee invasion had reached the Creek Nation five bands or camps of their warriors under as many sub-chiefs had been stationed in various parts of the country, ready on short notice, to be massed under the famous Talitchlechee, who lived in the vicinity of the present town of Dacula in Gwinnett County. That old hero being informed by the colonists that the war cloud had passed away, at once ordered four of the camps to disband; but to hold themselves in readiness for action in case of necessity. The fifth camp, consisting of about thirty men, under the sullen sub-chief, Yrtyrmyrmyrmysco, was located at Bohuron, now known as Oconee Heights in Clarke County. The leader of the Bohurons, as his followers were called, asked and received permission to remain in camp until it was known by better evidence than any white man could give that all danger was over. This slur together with the fact that none of the camps had been established near Fort Strong, nor on any part of Umausauga's claim, and also the emphasis placed on the last part of Talitchlechee's order disbanding the four camps, gave the colonists the first hint that there was an element of hostility among some of the natives around them. Though they said nothing, they "trusted in God and kept their powder dry."

Umausauga was a strong, brave man. He knew by instinct that "coming events cast their shadows before them." He seems to have had a bad opinion of the leader of the Bohurons from the beginning. He knew that the chief had been spurned as a viper by his darling Banna, and that it was natural for one of his race to seek revenge. Really he more than half believed that the negigole (renegade) remained in the country for that purpose.

For Umausauga to think was to do. As soon as the camp was established under the long-named chief, he induced Tata, his nephew at Snodon, to change his name to Nyxter, and join the Bohurons as a spy. Though not fully grown Tata was a strong, sharp young fellow, and little known outside of his secluded home circle. He was known to be fearless, faithful and true to his friends. His skill with the bow was unerring and his fleetness on foot was superior to that of the red deer.

A few days after the four camps disbanded it was reported that the Bohurons had gone south to join the Lower Creeks to which their leader really belonged. Hence Umausauga's term of derision, *negigole*. Had he known a stronger term he certainly would have used it. Though often asked to live at the fort, he continued to stay in his wigwam at night and to roam the woods by day. He knew nothing of the sensation of fear, though, to use his own expression, he "walked with his eyes looking and slept with his ears hearing."

As if to prove this saying, he one night heard the preconcerted signal of Nyxter, the spy. They met at the appointed place where some startling revelations were made. The boy informed his uncle that the southward movement of the Bohurons was only a ruse; that half of the company was still in camp and would remain there as a blind. That the other half which had gone south would return in a short time and watch the woods by day and the fort by night for an opportunity to capture both Banna and Ruth Lahgoon and carry them away to the Lower Creeks; that Wogolog was a leading Bohuron and wanted revenge for the way Ruth received his advances at Calamit; that Yrtyrmyrmyrmysco was still determined to make Banna his wife, and that he had sworn vengeance against Josiah Strong as the only cause of his rejection.

"I am on fire all over, and will see about that matter before the moon shines on my tracks," said the furious Indian as he hastened away to Fort Strong. Quickly reaching there he told the startling news and Mr. Easley, who was president of the council at the time, quietly asked: "What is the best thing for us to do?" "I want two arrows unlike any ever used in this part of the country. Will you help me make them?" was the equally quiet reply. "I think you need not make any. I have a small bundle of those that were used in King Phillip's war," said Joe Starr, as he went to get them. "These," he continued upon his return, "were given to me by my father. They are called King Phillip arrows, and I value them very highly. Still you are welcome to two or three if they suit you."

Umausauga took the bundle eagerly and critically examined the arrows one by one. The shafts were unusually long and made of a tough, fine-grained wood unknown to the Creek or to any of the colonists. The tips or heads were made of a very dark flint, and tapered to a long, keen point. The Indian's eyes sparkled with delight as he selected two and returned the others.

"Now," he said as he arose to go, "hide the others where they cannot be seen by prying eyes," and thanking Joe for the favor, he disappeared in the reigning darkness.

The following day and night were uneventful, but during the evening of the second day seven or eight Bohurons were seen to enter the dense woods to the south of Alotha, and were supposed to be heading for the deep ravine which still distinguishes that locality. This proximity to the fort was rather ominous; but to be forewarned was to be forearmed, and everything was in order there. For the first time Umausauga and his brother, Etohautee of Snodon, remained at the fort all night. About break of day the latter, who was patrolling the immediate vicinity with the stealthiness of a mousing cat, saw the enemy cross the river and go in the direction of the Okoloco Trail. A few hours later the white men, leaving the Indian brothers as a guard, left the fort on a tour of observation. When the little company reached the trail the fresh tracks of fast runners going east were soon discovered. Presently another runner was seen coming at full speed; but as soon as he saw the white men he dashed into the woods. It was the work of a few minutes only for Mr. Lahgoon, who was mounted on Alborak, to overtake him. When brought back he refused to speak, but soon found it was easier to talk than to die. He said his chief had been killed and his men were scattered in every direction; that Wogolog, the next in command, was very sick and that he had been carried to the low country to be treated by a famous doctor down there.

The captain then led the way to his fallen chief who was found lying near Calamit with an arrow buried deep in his head. It was a King Phillip arrow, in all probability the first of its kind that ever cleared the air in that part of the country. And yet the white men knew that Umausauga had not sent it on its deathly mission. When they approached the dead leader three men were sitting near, apparently expecting the arrival of others. Not one of the natives spoke a word or moved a muscle. When asked if they needed help one of the sullen warriors shook his head and pointed down the trail, as much as to say that help was expected from that direction.

A few days after the death of Yrtyrmyrmyrmysco, two old men visited Adabor. They carried with them the spearless shaft of the King Phillip arrow. Having entered the head a little in front of the right ear, it had been sped with such force that when pulled away the spear remained in the bones of the skull. The object of the visit was to know if Umausauga had ever seen such an arrow used by either Upper Creek or Cherokee. He had never seen one used, and promptly answered in the negative; but suggested that such deadly missiles might be used by Lower Creeks who live on the coast.

"That," said one of the old men, "may be true. Yrtyrmyrmyrmysco has enemies there. Some of them have followed him and sent this arrow almost through his head. What a true bowman the fellow is!" "Yes," said Umausauga to himself after the old men went away, "that fellow happened to be Tata Nyxter, as true a bowman as ever let an arrow fly! It is a pity that he can not use the other now. But look out, Wokolog! It's not too late yet!"

Following the death of the leader of the Bohurons and the disappearance of his lieutenant, the Talasee colony slept soundly once more.

A short distance above the mouth of Sandy Creek there was small lagoon or shallow lake, surrounded by a dense growth of cane, briers and other small swamp growth. On its north side was a slightly elevated plot of dry land on which stood a little hut made of poles and covered with canes and clay mortar. As a Bohuron Tata Nyxter was well acquainted with the ground, knew the purposes of the hut and the exact location of the only path that led to it. When passing on his way to Notha Neva's home in the almost interminable wilderness which lay a short distance east of the creek, he noticed that the path had been traveled recently. At first he thought it only a common occurrence and passed on. But knowing that the path led to the "Secret Council Chamber" of the Bohurons, the further he went the more he became convinced that in all probability something unusual was on hand. Hastening on he told his host of the discovery made, and was informed that strangers had been recently seen going towards the swamp beyond the creek on several different occasions.

Even against the advice of his friends, he resolved to investigate the matter that very night. He knew that if the strangers were Bohuron leaders, they would sleep in the hut until about midnight, and broil their meat and talk over their plans before daylight. Resolving that if discovered he would claim the rights of the clan himself (for the use he had made of King Phillip's arrow was still unknown to any besides the few who knew the secret even before the deed was done), the boy reached the path leading to hut awhile before midnight.

Judging that the coast was clear, he crawled upon his hands and knees near the hut and concealed himself in a cluster of scrubby laurel that grew near the lake and between it and the hut, wisely thinking that no one would be likely to come or go in that direction.

By and by someone was heard snoring in the hut and the spy knew it was inhabited. He thought it the loudest snoring he had ever heard, and presently another, evidently annoyed at the discordant sound said snappishly: "Huh! Huh! Huh! Up wake! you the country alarm!"

A long-drawn yawn was heard, and the snoring ceased. A long talk followed of which the spy barely heard enough to convince him that his suspicions were well founded. Soon, however, a light appeared in the hut, and the boy knew that meant broiling meat, roasting an ash cake. Silently stealing near, he looked through a small opening in the wall and saw two men sitting near the fire broiling bear meat. The odor was delightful, yet he dared do nothing but look and listen.

One of the men was Wokolog, a well-known Bohuron leader, who, of all Indians, Tata Nyxter and his father most hated. The other was a stranger dressed in skin decorated with bear and eagle claws. On his head was sort of skullcap from which protruded quite an array of fine feathers (Ostrich), of a kind the spy has never seen before. This indicated that the stranger was from a distance. Really he was a fine looking fellow of medium size, whose features, form, dress and movements strongly reminded one of Yrtyrmyrmyrmysco.

Few words were spoken while the meat was cooking; but soon as it was taken off the coals the men engaged in conversation.

From all that was said the stealth listener learned that the stranger's name was Bonoaguartah, brother of the slain Bohuron chief, and that his presence in the country was to reorganize that clan and avenge the death of his brother. That as the curious arrow that killed the chief must have been furnished or used by some pale-face, any white man or woman, not even excepting the royal blooded Banna, or any Indian friendly to the whites, should be the object of their vengeance, and that they would be ready to start upon the war path at half of this moon.

As the new moon went down a little after dark that night, "at half of this moon" meant about thirteen days hence. As was afterwards learned nearly two weeks were allowed so as to give recruits expected from the low country time to arrive.

Having gained this startling information, Tata looked at the stars, and finding that daybreak was near, hastened away as he had come. Soon he and Notha Neva was on a brisk run for Snodon, which accounts for their early arrival there.

Arrangements were made at once to inform all the citizens of Beadland and of Talasee, Fort Yargo, Thomocoggan, Yamacutah and Groaning Rock colonies of the impending danger. The bearer of the news to each place carried a written message of which the following is a copy:

"Georgia, Franklin Co.
"Snodon, Aug. 8th, 1795

"To the Colonies of Yamacutah.
"Dear Friends:

"Danger threatens. We have lots of dry powder. If necessary come help us burn it. Bearer will give particulars. Hurrah for success.   Devotedly,

"Helen Draper."

As the time for Mino's departure was at hand, he took affectionate leave of his relatives and their friends saying: "If danger comes Mino will be with you. He too knows how to use the cracking rifle as well as the twanging bow."

Accompanied by Notha Neva, each carrying a turkey, the brothers left Snodon with some sadness. As messengers of the people of Beadland, they went by the way of Thomocoggan, Yamacutah and Groaning Rock.

The colonists being already well provided with arms and ammunition, the next thing deemed necessary was an effective organization. They could, all told, muster a force of 98 fighting white men, and about half that number of women, many of them, perhaps all, being as heroic in case of necessity as Helen Draper herself. Besides all of them, including Nyrulyn and Mera, were dead shots, and as effective at the port hole and sometimes in the open field as any man.

After an absence of a few days which Umausauga has spent among his personal friends, he returned with 17 loyal followers, which, when added to the proscribed Indians, Umausauga, Etohautee, Tata Nyxter, Hoochlechoopah and Notha Neva made a fighting contingent of 22 friendly natives, making a total of 120 available men. Besides, if the fight continued to be a local one as was supposed, they expected valuable aid from their sister colonies.

About ten days before the expected outbreak an organization was effected which proved satisfactory to all.

Johnson Josiah Strong was elected Commander-in-Chief, and the white men, being divided into 1st, 2nd, and 3rd companies, Joe Lavender, Ed Damron and Abe Trent were their commanders, with the rank of Captain. Ocean Scupeen was quickly selected patrolling scout.

Umausauga was placed over the natives with Tata Nyxter patrolling scout. To complete the organization Helen Draper was elected viva voce to lead the women, with rank of Captain.

To show the spirit of that girl more fully it may be said that after her election she stepped in front and said, "All commanders-in-chiefs have aides. I therefore appoint Banna de Vedo Strong, Marzee

Marcum, and Mera Hoochlechoopah my aides-de-camp. Comrades, take due notice thereof and govern yourselves accordingly, though I don't know just what that means. Hurrah for success."

"Hurrah for success," shouted all the men, and each one felt that a true Joan of Arc was among them. So far as doing anything the girl commander thought little of her shout, and less of her appointments at the time, but "Hurrah for success," became the battle cry of the colonists, and her aid did as much to achieve "success" as any other three soldiers in the field.

[The selections below give a history of Banna, Umausauga's adopted daughter, and her real parentage, and show the presence of Spanish among the native people of Georgia in the late 1700s.]

About sixteen years before the beginning of our narrative a war broke out between the Cherokee and Upper Creek Indians. The former claimed territory as far south as the Tishmaugu, and the latter as far north and east as the Lacoda Trail,* which was nearly identical with the present Athens and Clarkesville road. Their first engagement was at Numerado, near the confluence of Hurricane Creek and Etoho river above Hurricane Shoals. Amercides, apparently an Indian with a Greek name, was leader of the Cherokees, and as gallant a brave as ever drew a bow. He rode a white horse and dashed from place to place as if trained on the battlefields of Europe.

Talitchlechee, commander of the Creeks, saw the mistake, and placing himself at a favorable point awaited the expected opportunity. It soon came and the Creek buried his tomahawk in the gallant leader's side. When the white horse was seen running riderless through the forest of Numerado, the Cherokees began to retreat. But soon the scene changed. Elancydyne, the wife or as she was generally called, the queen of Amercides, committing a small child that she was holding in her arms to the care of an attendant, mounted the riderless horse and at once took command. She was greeted by a yell from the Cherokees that echoed and re-echoed up and down the river and forward and back across the valley. Soon the air was thick with flying arrows and whizzing tomahawks.

The conflict deepened and the battle raged on. The commander was more cautious than her fallen lord, but rode unflinchingly in the face of every danger. At last the Creeks, finding their ranks so fatally thinned, retreated hastily. Another yell—this time the yell of victory, reverberated over the hills, and the heroine of the day, forgetting all things else, hastened to see if her child was safe. She found it sleeping soundly in the arms of her attendant, who, to shield the babe from harm, had received an arrow deeply in her shoulder. Her name was Yetha, and though the wound was thought to be fatal, she lived to be very old.

Soon a band of young warriors gathered around the queen, and carrying her over the battlefield, in grim mockery introduced her to the fallen Creeks as their conqueror—their beautiful Elancydyne.

Elated with their decisive victory the Cherokees considered the country conquered territory as far as they claimed and began a march across it to take formal possession. In the meantime, however, the Creeks had received substantial recruits, and Talitchlechee being a wily old chief of long experience, the enterprise was doubtful. His enemy, still led by what her followers considered their invincible new queen, moved slowly and cautiously forward until they reached the verge of the plateau which dips to Cold Spring, then known as Rodoata, near the John Harrison old place, where they met Talitchlechee in command of a larger force than at Numerado.

The Creeks gave the gage of battle and soon the engagement became general. Though queen Elancydyne showed that she was a skillful and fearless leader, she was finally overcome by numbers, and by a master piece of strategy made a flank movement, and going still forward, camped that night at Arharra on the plain where Prospect Church now stands and within hearing of the waters of the Tishmaugu, the object of her expedition. This singular movement on the part of an enemy which had shown such consummate skill so puzzled Talitchlechee that he hesitated to offer battle as he had down at Rodoata. The next morning, however, an accident brought on a general engagement with varying success. This continued at intervals until noon when the Creek chief sent Umausauga, one of his trusted braves, to conceal a number of expert bowmen in the branches of some spreading trees that grew in an adjacent forest. Late in the afternoon the conflict again became general.

Elancydyne on her white horse led the van, and her example so inspired her followers that they gave another deafening yell and rushed forward to engage at close quarters; but the Creeks retreated in the direction of the concealed bowmen. Again the Cherokee queen was in the thickest of the fray and soon fell from her horse pierced by many bristling arrows. The wail of lament, "Onocowah, Onocowah!" rising from the field of carnage, disheartened the Cherokees, and they in turn sullenly retreated to the north, tenderly carrying their fallen queen with them. If she had survived the battle it is difficult to say what would have been the result.

[Banna, Umausauga's daughter, and Ruth, a white woman, visit Lapsidali]

Notwithstanding the number of brave, strong men belonging to the colony, Banna the Beautiful and Ruth Lahgoon the Lovely, were appointed scouts to patrol the surrounding country. All the men were needed for heavy work; besides none were better that these two brave and skillful riders. A few days of instruction by Mr. Strong had enabled them to converse with each other readily, and they had become equal experts with the rifle. They generally went together and always in hearing of each other. As a protection to the women and children, the dogs, Pyth and Damon, were left at home. Both wore deerskin clothing, made to fit closely, and jaunty little caps of the same material from which generally fluttered a short black ribbon. They carried comparatively light rifles, and on the left breast of each the hilt of a deadly stiletto was just visible.

Thus equipped and mounted on Alborak and Iro, these scouts fearlessly roamed the forests infested with dangerous wild beasts and sometimes with wilder men. They met with many adventures, some of which it is necessary to give here...

Seminole Warrior on Horse

Photo of Paul "Swamp Owl" Morrison, courtesy of the Seminole Tribe of Florida

On the morning following the above-mentioned meeting the scouts crossed the river and rode to the west. As Ruth had formerly traveled in that direction, she knew that the country was rough and infested with dangerous animals. Therefore they rode near together, generally in single file, without meeting with anything unusual until they reached the lower water of Taurulaboole (Beech) creek. There as they entered the dense forest that skirted its banks, they discovered a little path that led to a cluster of tall reeds that grew on the knoll a short distance from the stream. Following the path they soon reached a curious structure almost hidden by the reeds which grew close to its walls. As they went near an opening which seemed to serve the purpose of a door, a wizen-faced old man made his appearance at the opening with a small bundle of split reeds in his hand. He had never seen two such beings before, and as they approached nearer he disappeared in the hut. However, when Banna told him in his own language that no harm was intended, an old squaw came to the door cautiously. She brought a half-finished basket in one hand and an old, rusty tomahawk in the other. She was hideous in appearance and evidently much older than the man. Her skin appeared to be dry on her bones, her great butter-teeth showed outside her thin, tightly drawn lips, and a tuft of hair, much like the foretop of a horse, fell straggling over her tawny brow. Banna at once recognized her as Lapsidali, a basket maker whom she had sometimes seen at Adabor.

Having long gazed with critical eyes at the girls and their horses, she laid down her basket and tomahawk on the ground and went nearer. When apparently satisfied that there was no danger, she went still nearer and patted Iro on the forehead. Ceasing to caress the horse, she looked up and carefully scanned the rider's features. Then she went backwards several steps, and placing both hands on her angular hips, she stood with a far-away look as if lost in some over-powering thought. Being unable to close her lips, they twitched over her great scurvy-eaten teeth as if talking to herself. Finally she suddenly turned and called to the little old man who was still in the hut, and said in substance:

"Onomaco, this girl on white horse is certainly Banna. Lives at Adabor, I have seen her there. But she has changed to butterfly. That's to keep Cherokees from knowing her. Two white horses. Two queens, too. This white horse like Adar. The other on black horse is pale face. Lives at Shoals. Flies through the air. Spirit floats up and down river every night. No harm in her. Come out here."

The old hag advanced to pat the black horse also. Somehow Alborak refused to be petted by her, and throwing back his ears, he gave a short, vicious snip at her arm. The old woman snatched up her tonahawk, and her movements indicated that she intended to throw it at the horse's head. Perhaps she did not know just what that meant, but at the click of the lock she fled into the hut and crouched beyond a pile of baskets.

[Huanaco, a Cherokee, comes to find out if Banna is really the child of Amercides and Elancydyne, and he addresses Umausauga, his dauhter, Banna, and friends of theirs]

In personal appearance, this Indian was far superior to any others seen in the country, and while he had the step and the hair peculiar to the natives, he did not resemble them in any other respects.

"Friends, many moons ago the Creeks and Cherokees were at war. We were led by King Amercides. He was a Spanish nobleman. For some reason he became one of us. He died for us on the bloody field of Numerado. Then his queen took his place. She led us to victory. Her name was Elancydyne. Though of pure English blood she was always true to the Cherokees. When a very little girl she was washed ashore by the waves of the sea. We adopted her and she too became one of us. She grew to be so good and beautiful that King Amercides gladly made her his queen. She led us from Numerado to other battlefields. The last was at Arharra near this very place. There, when passing under some trees in whose branches bowmen were hidden, she fell mortally wounded. The spirit of the Cherokees was broken. We retreated beyond the Etoho. We carried our queen's dead body with us. She and Amercides sleep together. After the battle we tried to find her little girl. She was the very image of her mother. Her name was Eltrovadyne. Until a short time ago we fully believed her to be dead. I have been sent to see if she still lives. I think I have found her. We want her for a queen. Friends," the Indian continued, after a thoughtful pause, "I was once wounded in battle. Queen Elancydyne poured cold water on a great gash in my shoulder. Her beautiful eyes looked on in pity. She, whom you call Banna gave me just such a look with just such eyes while pouring water on my arm to-night. The discovery overcame me. I fell upon the floor. I know that was not in keeping with the dignity of a warrior. But tell me, O tell me, if you can, is Banna, the once little queen Eltrovadyne? What shall Huanaco tell his people?"

[Banna speaks to Huanaco]

"Talk to Eltrovadyne," said Banna, wishing to turn the current of the Indian's thoughts. "Please tell me what Elancydyne means?" "Shooting Star," answered the Cherokee slowly, and again pointing upward, continued, "When Elancydyne was a little girl a Cherokee brave took her from a sinking ship in time of a storm, and the waves brought them both to shore. Later she ran about from one camp-fire to another so fast, and she was so very, very bright and beautiful, that she was called Elancydyne or Shooting Star. Our old men said her clothes showed that she was the child of an English nobleman. She was very white with features just like yours. O her eyes! O your eyes, Eltrovadine! How can I leave...

"May Eltrovadyne ask a few more questions?" The Indian nodded his head, and sat with eyes cast down as if to avoid the heartbreaking battery that was turned upon him. "What does Amercides mean?" asked the girl tremulously. "Don't know," was the thoughtful reply. "When your father first came among

110

the Cherokees he was known as Don Mar de Vedo, of the royal family of Spain. Huanaco don't remember all about it. He was then young. Something like CID was connected with his name. When he was made king his subjects were required to call him Amercides. So Cid was still part of his name."

[Banna's horse, and a description of a saddle that had been found in the woods, and was given to Banna by Umausauga]

"Iro was indeed a beautiful animal. Though not so large as Alborak, he was of good size, and as elegantly formed. He was a pure white except his mane and tail which were of a light canary hue. The yellow tint was afterwards found to be artificial; but it certainly enhanced the beauty of the animal, and was then as appropriate for a white horse as the painting of a lady's face is now. The training of Iro and Alborak was different; but the result was the same. The white came when his name was called, the black when he heard a peculiar whistle given by his mistress, and by her only.

Iro's equipment consisted of a bridle and a sidesaddle, both of Spanish make. From the right hand horn of the saddle hung a bow and a small quiver of arrows. It had no hoop, but a tomahawk of curious shape was tied to the rear. On the small right-hand skirt the flag of Spain was imprinted in good style. Beneath the flag was the following inscription: DON MAR DE VEDO X ELANCYDYNE.

On the morning following the memorable meeting of the Talasee council in which Banna unexpectedly learned much of her early history, her saddle was identified by Huanaco as the same on which queen Elancydyne rode over the battlefields of Numerado, Rodoata and Arharra. He said he distinctly remembered it as a gift from Amercides to his queen, and that the first journey made upon it was her ride from Shaultamoozaw (Black Creek church) to Yamtramahoochee (Hurricane Shoals) just before the battle of Numerado. Thus the parentage of the bright girl long known as Umausauga's daughter was established to the satisfaction of herself and her friends; and the declaration of Mrs. Moore that she did not have a drop of Indian blood in her was fully verified. Consequently her name was at once enrolled upon the records of Talasee council as Banna Mar de Vedo, the first name being retained because of its well-known significance.

[Umausauga gives Banna her mother's necklace on the occasion of her marriage]

Again the speaker paused for a short time and stood in anxious thought. Then suddenly thrusting his hand in his coat pocket he slowly drew out a long necklace of glittering pearls and sparkling diamonds...

"My lost daughter—I must still call you by that endearing name—this was your mother's necklace. You father gave it to her when he was made king of the Cherokees. As you know, he was killed at the battle of Numerado. Your mother quickly took his place. After mounting her white horse, Adar, she pulled off her necklace. She left it in the care of your nurse. It was stolen from her. Huanaco afterwards learned where the jewels were hidden. Soon after he left her he told Daxator your history. He was the chief who succeded your mother. He ordered Huanaco to take some men with him and bring both necklace and thief to headquarters. The order was soon executed. Daxator took possession of the treasure and punished the thief severely. Only a few days ago he sent the necklace to me. He instucts me to give it to you. So now, my darling daughter," he said as he raised the precious gift above her head, "I place this representative of royalty around your neck in the name of the Cherokee people. I have performed my mission. Umausauga is done."

CHAPTER SIX

Otras Palabras, Otras Tierras
Other Words, Other Lands

Other Words, Other Lands

The excerpts from "The Early History of Jackson County" concerning the Bohurons contain names that pique our interest, and a number of them can be found to be drawn from native languages, although changed through inaccurate transcription. Other words cannot be found in the usual sources, but have proven to be a reflection of the ethnic diversity that existed in the Jackson County area in the late eighteenth century. Whenever fitting, we have provided alternate explanations, as we did with words taken from the Nodoroc passages. As always, we have cast the broadest possible net.

Adar: Yet another horse. This horse is mentioned by Lapsidali in comparison with Alborak and Iro the horses belonging to Ruth and to Banna.

Adar is an Arabic word meaning "prince" or "noble."

Alotha: A place: Probably from Creek word, *elofa,* meaning "sole of foot."

Amercides Mar de Vedo: Banna's real father

There is a great mystery about the young woman, Banna, the child that Umausauga found after a battle and raised as his own. Some of the non-natives believe that she is white, because of her different features and wavy hair. A Cherokee named Juanaco appears, and tells that Banna is actually Eltrovadyne, the daughter of a Spanish nobleman, Don Mar de Vedo, who became leader of the Cherokee, and a white woman, Eltrovadyne, his queen. Mar de Vedo is a Spanish name, *mar* meaning "sea," and *Vedo* possibly a shortening of "Quevedo." (The famous Golden Age writer, Francisco de Quevedo, was a descendant of Castilian nobility).

In "The Early History of Jackson County," Huanaco talks of Banna's real father, being made chief of the Cherokees: "Something like CID was connected with his name. When he was made king his subjects were required to call him Amercides. So Cid was still part of his name."

In Arabic, *Amir* or *Ameer*, means "prince," "commander."

In Arabic *sayyid* means liege-lord, from that comes *sidi*—"my liege."

Similarly, in Spanish, *Cid* indicates someone of noble birth, doubtlessly derived from the Arabic.

It makes perfect sense that Don Mar de Vedo would require his "subjects" to address him as "Prince, my liege."

The name exists today as Arabic surnames such as Hamersid and Amirsaeedi.

The presence of Don Mar de Vedo shows that other ethnic groups had been assimilated into the Cherokee tribes living in the area.

Bohuron: The Bohurons were a warlike branch of the Creeks. Bohuron is also the name of the place, now Oconee Heights, where the Bohurons lived.

1. *Bohuron* derives from an Arabic word.

Collectanea de Rebus Hibernicus: Vallancey, C.
The Uraikeft, Or Book of Oghams
(Collection of Irish Matters)

This book, published in Dublin in 1790, which talks about how Southern Scythians made their way to Spain then to Ireland, contains a section on Irish Brehon-Amhan (Breithamhuin) laws, and defines many terms. So according to this, "Bohuron" has no Gaelic origin, but a Gaelic law term, "Boaire," has it's origins in the arabic word, *bohur*.

On page 237 (Law Glossary) is the Irish term of law, "Boaire":
Boaire, a degree of nobility. Arab. *bohur, bohuron,*
vir liberalis

2. A Breton surname is another possibility.

3. It could also derive from a place name. Navarre was an independent Protestant kingdom until 1620. It is on the border between France and Spain. Until 1620, it also included much of Gascony. Navarese and Gascon are dialects of a unique language that blend Celtic, Basque, Spanish and French.

King Henry of Navarre became King of France in 1594, but was killed by a fanatic in 1610. His Catholic wife immediately began repressing the French Huguenots. In 1620, Spain overran the southern 2/3 of Navarre and sent in the Inquisition. Those Protestants were not burned at the stake fled for their lives to any non-Catholic country they could find. The Protestants in Gascony were not treated much better. The ocean was the easiest escape. It is possible that Navarese and Gascon refugees ended up in the Georgia & North Carolina mountains since many of the original explorers of the Georgia Mountains were French Protestants. Bohuron may be derived from a district in Gascony with a similar name.

On a 1771 Map of Guyenne and Gascony:
La Bouhaire, a town in the western mountain ranges. The town is south of Bourdelois, and northwest of D'Albert. Town is now called Labouheyre.

Bonoaguartah/ brother of Yrtyrmyrmyrmysco
Bono suggests "good," *bueno* in Spanish, *bom* in Portuguese.

Aguartah has the sound of *aguarda*, from Portuguese *aguardar*, to wait; or *guardar*, to guard, to protect.

Guarda is also a Portuguese Serphardic surname, after the name of a city in Portugal founded in the 12th century.

This name comes from the Spanish/Portugues, and most probably Sephardic, showing, once again, the presence of Sephardic Jews.

Daxator: A Cherokee who took over as chief after the deaths of Amercides and Elancydine
Daxator has been seen as a name in the Oneida and Mohawk tribes, so is most likely Iroquoian in origin. Daxator may have entered the tribe through a slave raid and later been accepted among the Cherokees as one of their own; or perhaps his parents or grandparents had.

Elancydine and Eltrovadyne: Elancydine, (also *Elancydyne*)a Cherokee Queen married to Don Mar de Vedo; Eltrovadyne, her daughter, known as Umausauga's adopted daughter, Banna.
Both these names sound moorish. "El" is a common Arabic prefix meaning "the." A name example would be *Elmira*, an arabic girl's name meaning "the lady," or "the princess."

Din (also ad-Din) is an arabic suffix meaning "of the religion," (referring to divine law, or *Shari'a*), or simple "faith." A familiar example would be *Aladdin*.

Eltrovadine: "Trova" may be from the Spanish or Portuguese word for verse or poem, *trova*, which comes from the word *trovador* meaning troubadour.

Ancy from Elancydine may have some relation to the Spanish word *anciano*, meaning old or ancient.

Etoho River – from Creek word *Etvlwv*, which means "Etowah River."

Hoochlechoopah: a Creek Indian – from Creek words, Hvcci-Chvpv.

Huanaco: A Cherokee brave who comes to verify reports that Eltrovatine (Banna), the queen's daughter, is alive.

Juanaco is a Spanish or Portuguese hypocoristic, or nickname, form of Juan. Examples of hypocoristic names from Juan are: *Juanca* or *Juanqui* for Juan Carlos; *Juanvi* for Juan Vicente; and *Juancris* for Juan Cristóbal. It is likely that *Juanaco* it is a familiar form of *Juan Acco, Acco* meaning "Jacob." This would be a strong indication of a Sephardic Jewish background. *Acco* is also a Sephardic surname.

Also, there is very striking is the description of Juanaco in "The Early History of Jackson County" :
"In personal appearance this Indian was far superior to any others seen in the country, and while he had the step and the hair peculiar to the natives, he did not resemble them in any other respects."

This adds more credence to the idea that his Cherokee tribe contained an ethnic mix.

Lacoda Trail :
> Most likely this word is derived from the Iberian or Ladino proper noun, *La Cota*, meaning "elevation."

Negigole: Umausauga uses the term to refer to Yrtyrmyrmyrmysco, saying it means "renegade," because he is a Lower Creek.
> This probably comes from Apalachicola Creek words, *Neke-kola*, meaning shaking people or people moving back and forth.

Nyxter: A name given by Umausauga to his nephew Tata so that he could infiltrate the Bohuron camp. The Dutch name *Nijster* has a sound almost identical to Nyxter. It can also be spelled. *Nijsters, Nejster, Knijsters, Neij-starr, Najster*, etc, but most commonly Nijster, sometimes with an "s" on the end, sometimes not. There are records of families named Nijsters traveling in the 1800s from Eastern Europe listed as Jews. There were also listings for Nijsters in the East India Company in the 1700s out of Holland. Many Jews from Spain and Portugal found refuge in The Netherlands, particularly Amsterdam.

One significant note: Umausauga chose this name for his nephew in order that he could go live among the Bohurons in order to spy. We have to assume that he would have chosen a name that would fit in and be accepted. This suggests a Dutch and/or Sephardic presence was not uncommon.

Okoloco Trail: From Itsate Creek, *Oka-loco,* meaning "Water Big."

Shultamoozaw: An Indian village
> *Shultam* is listed in the lineage of Elisha in the Stories of the Prophets in the Quran. The word ending seems Portuguese; probably *ção*, which would have that nasal "zaow" sound.

Snodon: A town - *Snowdon* – Wales highest mountain - Old English for "snow hill"

Taurulaboole: A stream – from Itsate Creek words, *Tvlula Pvle*, meaning, "Town Round." Some branches of the Creek pronounce an "l" as a rolling "r" sound.

Tishmaugu, A stream – from an Itsate Creek word, *Tis-mako*, which means "Servant of the King." It is also similar to a Chickasaw word, meaning the same thing.

Wogolog: Next in command in the Bohurons.
Wakalat is a muslim name meaning "helper" or "assistant," and on page 108 of "The History of Jackson County," we read: "Wogolog was a leading Bohuron..." This would seem to bolster the possibility that *Bohuron* is itself an Arabic word, meaning "nobility."

Yrtyrmyrmyrmysco: The leader of the Bohurons
It's most likely that this spelling is similar to the name's actual sound, but not exact.
The first two syllables, Yr-tyr, could be an attempt to capture the Arabic word Altair, meaning, "bird," or "one that flies." In Arabic, the pronunciation is closer to "A-ta-ir."

That leaves us with myr-myr-misco.

In Arabic, *Mir*, is derived from *Amir* or *Ameer*, meaning "prince," or "commander."
See "Amercides," above

Another familiar feature is that *–isco* is a common Spanish and Portuguese suffix denotes "like," or "in the manner of." The equivalent in English would be *—esque*, as in *romanesque*.

CHAPTER SEVEN

Yamacutah, El Misterio

Yamacutah, The Mystery

YAMACUTAH

Richard Thornton
Architect & City Planner

Virtual reality image by Richard Thornton, Architect

"...by mutual consent of all the tribes the life of neither beast or bird, nor
any living thing, should ever perish there. It was ever to be a place of refuge
and never to have upon it the stain of blood."

Yamacutah

Excerpt from

The Early History of Jackson County, Georgia

In 1784 Jordan Clark and Jacob Bankston, two enterprising and adventurous young men, came from Virginia to Wilkes County, Georgia. There they met with a roving band of Choctaw Indians who told them of a strange old camping-ground which they called Yamacutah. They said it was located on the banks of Etoho (Oconee) river, some two days' journey toward the setting sun; that the Great Spirit once lived there; and that since his disappearance Indians sometimes went to the place to walk the paths which God once trod, and then hastened away, as He had done, without leaving a trail to show which way they went.

Having their curiosity aroused, Clark and Bankston at once resolved to go and see if the Choctaws had told them the truth. Late on the afternoon of April 22, 1784, they reached a series of small shoals, which they immediately recognized as Yamacutah. While the stream was small and the shoals modest, they were curious, and their surroundings were sublime and awe-inspiring far beyond anything known to the present inhabitants.

Trees of fabulous dimensions interlocked their ponderous branches, and the acorns and chestnuts of the previous year literally covered the ground. The glaring eyes and startling bound of the red deer, the wild chattering of a multitude of birds, and the warning signal of the rattlesnake, told the newcomers that such beings had seldom, if ever, been there before.

Distant some twenty yards, a great black bear was perched in the fork of a tree. As he moved his forepaws with the evident intention of descending, a ball from Clark's deadly rifle crashed through his head. Curious to say, as we afterwards learned, that bear's life was the first ever known to be taken at or near Yamacutah. After a "delightful supper of broiled bear ham," as the adventurers described it, they slept by turns, through most of the night, and with the rising sun began a careful examination of their surroundings.

About seventy-five yards from the west end of the natural rock dam they discovered a curious upright statue a little over four feet high. It was made of a soft talcose rock, 13 inches square at the bottom; but the top, from the shoulders up, was a fair representation of a human figure. The shoulders were rudimentary, but he head was well formed. The neck was unduly long and slender. The chin and forehead were retreating. The eyes were finely executed, and looked anxiously to the east. It stood at the center of an earth mound (17) seventeen feet in circumference and six feet high. Around it were many other mysteries which will never be fully explained. Only a few of them may be mentioned now.

Four paths, doubtless the ones the Choctaws mentioned, led, with mathematical precision, from the base of the mound to the cardinal points of the compass. Though it seemed that no other part of the forest had been trodden by human feet, these paths were as smooth and clean as a parlor floor. The scrubby cane, which seemed to have been planted by design along their margins, was as neatly trimmed as if the work had been done by a professional gardener. And here, amid those gloomy solitudes the natives believed that our God, their Great Spirit, had walked as a man walks along his homeward pathway.

The statue was found to be the center of an exact circle about one hundred and fifty yards in diameter. Its boundary was plainly marked by holes in the ground three feet apart. The holes to which the path ran in a straight line from the center were much larger than the intervening ones; and before them, inside the circle, were what seemed to be stone altars of varying dimensions. At the end of the path running to the north was a single triangular stone; at the east were five square stones and four steps; at the west, four stones and three steps; at the south, three stones and two steps. Upon the upper surface of all the stones except that at the north the effect of fire was plainly visible and doubtless had been used for sacrificial purposes.

All the paths terminated at the altars except the one running to the east. At this the trail parted, and, uniting beyond it, continued a short distance and then, much like an ascending column of smoke, disappeared, gradually. The account given by the Choctaws was verified. On the smooth surfaces of these stones were deeply cut both three and five-pointed half moons, whose horns turned different ways.

A good representation of the rising sun and other curious characters were deeply cut on the eastern altar.

Outside the circle were many ash heaps, beaten hard by the heavy hand of time, and over some of them were growing gigantic oaks and towering pines, as if to mark the grave of the dead past.

Having studied these and other features of the vicinity, the adventurers went back to their starting point with a determination to return and make a permanent settlement at Yamacutah.

For an unknown period of time the immediate territory on both sides of the river and for about one mile below, and to the Hurricane Shoals above, was neutral ground, claimed by neither Creek nor Cherokee, the lords of the adjoining territory.

For reasons already given it was considered Holy Ground: The Indian's Palestine. If on the war path, they went around it; if enemies met there they became friends as long as they remained there; by mutual consent of all the tribes the life of neither beast or bird, nor any living thing, should ever perish there. It was ever to be a place of refuge and never to have upon it the stain of blood. The killing of the bear by Clark was the first breach of law in the Holy Ground, and led, a few years later to open hostilities between the red and white men who lived in this part of the country.

On the 20th day of the following June Clark and Bankston returned to Yamacutah and began the first permanent settlement of white people within the present limits of Jackson County. They were accompanied by John Harris, a nephew of Nancy Hart, of revolutionary fame, and who became extensively known as Black Harris. He was a skillful workman in both wood and iron, and of almost unlimited resources in strategy and cunning.

A small cabin, which at once became dwelling-house and work-shop, was soon completed. Here such articles were made as seemed necessary to their simple wants. I now have a cupboard which was made by John Harris in that shop in 1785. It was made of boards split from a huge pine tree that grew upon an ash heap near the eastern altar. Though one hundred and twenty-one years old, it is still solid in all its points, and no modern mechanic can excel the workmanship.

This ancient "dresser," as the maker called it, together with a curious cluster of pine cones that grew upon the tree of which is was made; an acorn which fell from an oak that reached its ponderous branches far over the talcose statue; and some other things, I keep as mementoes of the shadowy past. When in want of curious mental food, or a desire to leap at a single bound from the present back to the long-gone past, I look at these relics of a former age. and with the old Saxon poet who, after his failure to penetrate the future, cried out: "ROLL BACK! ROLL BACK! Oh, wheels of time, roll back ! and let me realize something of the difference between then and now. "

The following year, 1785, was a memorable one. In May there came a cold wave which killed many large trees. The bird family was almost exterminated, and a large eagle, accidentally feeling the warmth of the cabin, became domesticated and remained a pet for several months, when it left wearing a bell which John Harris had fastened around its neck with his name and date engraved upon it. In 1790 this romantic bird was killed in the vicinity of Augusta. Even so large and hardy animals as wolves and panthers were found dead in the forest, and many fish were frozen in solid ice.

But the most remarkable phenomenon of that, or perhaps of any other year since the crufixion of the Son of God was the Dark Day on November 24th. It has never been explained, and the splendid illumination of the 20th century casts no light upon the cause of the darkness. Though the sun was visible all day long, and appeared to be much larger than usual, it omitted no light except such as may be seen while passing through a dense fog at night. The whole of animated nature on the Western Hemisphere was astonished on that day, and all who had ever heard of the final judgment listened in anxious expectation of hearing the long-drawn blasts of Gabriel's trumpet to wake the sleeping dead.

But only that which took place at Yamacutah concerns us now, and the tenth of that can not be told here. Even such strong and heroic men as Clark, Bankston and Harris were anxious, talked in whispers, and sat by their cabin all day. Various animals passed by in utter confusion, and several opossums and raccoons crouched near them, and though they sat with rifles across their knees, not a gun was fired the whole long day.

During the day many Indians came, and seating themselves around the mystic circle, gazed steadfastly towards the central figure. This they continued all day, and perhaps all night; for when next morning they saw the sun rise bright and golden as ever, they arose as one man, went inside the circle, and solemnly walking along the path to a step as regular as the beating of a healthy heart, they disappeared beyond the eastern altar as already indicated.

This was the last time this curious performance ever took place at the Tumbling Shoals, or anywhere else so far as I ever heard. What did it mean? Was there any more in it than a mere heathen ceremony ?

Final Thoughts on Yamacutah

In this chapter, Wilson recounts the narrative of Jordan Clark and Jacob Bankston whose 1784 visit to the area inspired them to establish a settlement near the present-day site of Maysville, in Jackson County, Georgia. Their description of the ceremonial site is so detailed and precise, that there can be no doubt that the account is authentic.

One can only imagine what these two young men must have felt when they found the statue with its long neck and retreating forehead. It must have been like nothing else that had ever seen. They could not have known that similar statues would be found the next century. In Monumental Remains of Georgia, author Charles Colcock Jones describes one such find near an earthen mound in Georgia. Although the description is much more detailed, it suggests a kinship with the statue found by Clark and Bankston.

> "Stone Idol._—This interesting relic, made of a coarse, dark sand-stone, is twelve inches in height. It consists of a human figure in a sitting posture, the knees drawn up, almost upon a level with the chin, the hands resting upon either knee, retreating chin and forehead—full head of hair, gathered into a knot behind—face upturned—eyes angular. Not a single feature, not a single idea connected with this image, is Indian in character. Everything about it—the place where it was exhumed—its internal evidence—all suggest the belief that it must have been fashioned by the ancient Mound-Builders." (page 109)[1]

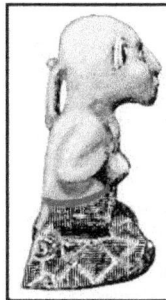

Above: Statues similar to one described by Jones, and to the statue at Yamacutah

Statue at Yamacutah

Virtual reality images by Richard Thornton, Architect

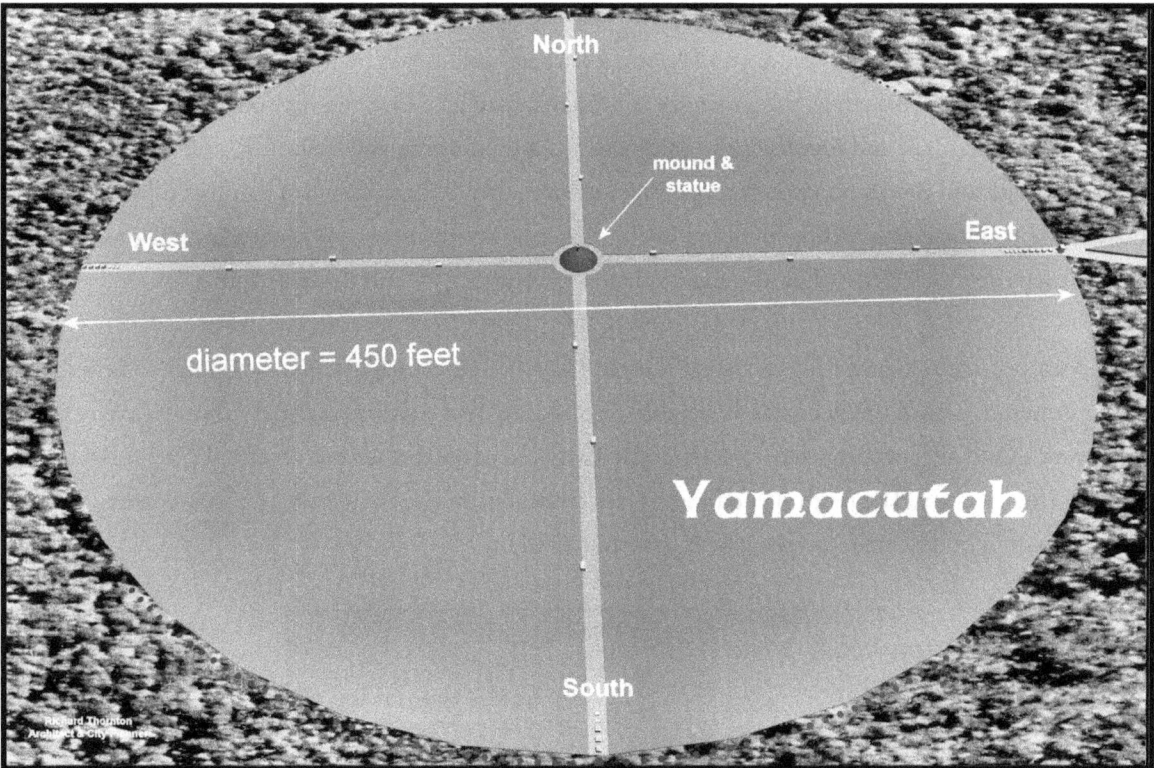

North

mound &
statue

West   East

diameter = 450 feet

Yamacutah

South

The Dimensions of Yamacutah

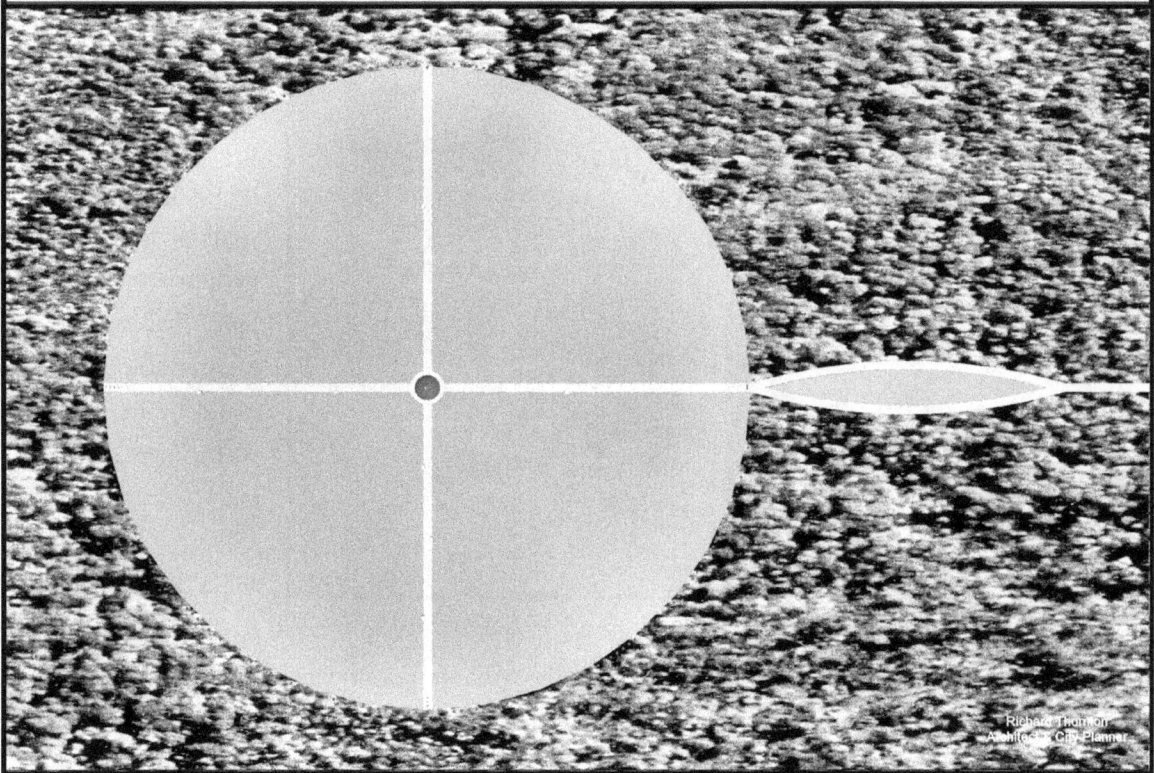

Clark and Bankston must have felt as if they had stepped into an ancient past. They must have stood in even greater awe when they began to walk along a curving path made by post holes, and slowly realized that the holes described a circle, the enormity of which is hard to conceive even today: A circle with a diameter of four hundred and fifty feet; and in its exact center, the strangely beautiful, east-facing statue on a mound. Clark and Bankston knew to expect a Holy site—the Indians they had met had told them it was such; but if, in addition to feeling humbled by the scale of such a place—and it's hard to imagine they wouldn't have felt humbled—they also felt a spiritual reverence. We can never be sure.

It's important to note that during the late 1700s and first half of the 1800s, it was popular to believe that Native Americans were intellectually incapable of building towns and pyramidal mounds, even though there were abundant European accounts from the Early Colonial Period that observed Native Americans living in these towns. The myth helped justify the treatment of the indigenous people as being sub-humans, who did not deserve to own the land that they lived on.

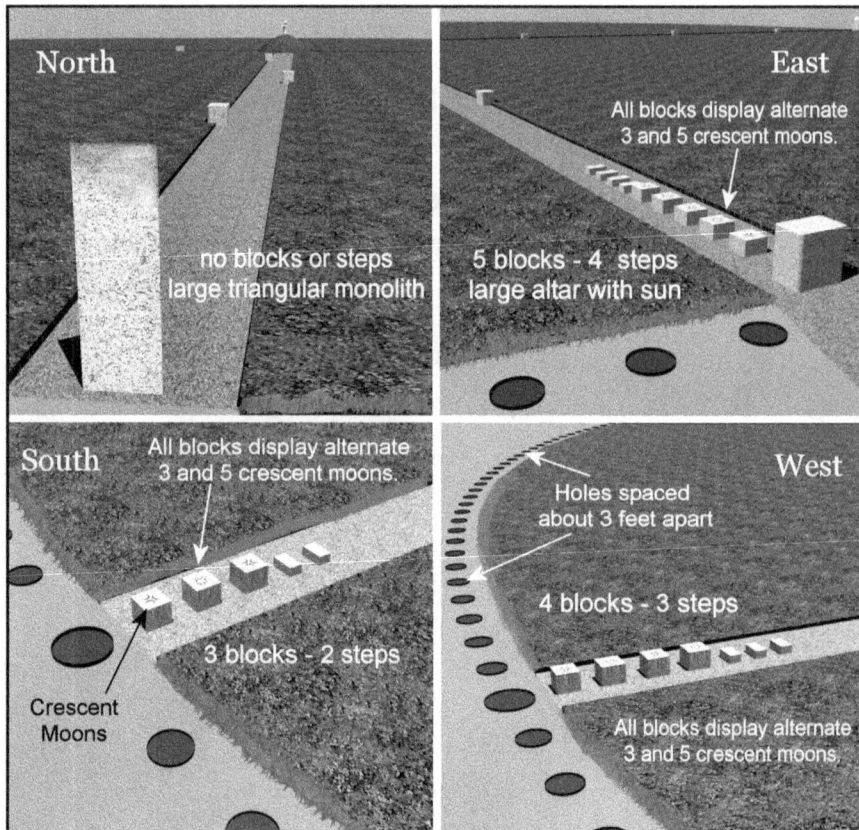

The Holiness of Yamacutah may explain why the site was seemingly unknown before Clark and Bankston's visit: It was simply too sacred, too important, and must have been a place which the Indians kept to themselves. Natives went there to trace the path where the Great Spirit had walked, "as a man walks," and there could be no room for white men and women.

In 1784, when Jordan Clark and Jacob Bankston were directed to Yamacutah, over two centuries of contacts with whites and their religions, had changed the relationship of many native peoples to their traditions. The Indians who told the two young travelers of "a strange old camping ground," seemed to have been removed from the beliefs associated with it. Yamacutah may have been as much a curiosity to them as it was to Clark and Bankston. (The narrative states that they were Choctaw, but it much more likely that they were Chickasaw, since the nearest Choctaw settlement would have been more than three hundred miles to the west. A band of Chickasaws lived only about thirty miles north of Yamacutah.

The men decided that they would settle in the area, and returned in June. Their first year near Yamacutah, though, was a strange one. The spring of 1785 was notable for a dramatic cold wave that killed many birds. But this part of Georgia was not the only place touched by severe weather. In fact, the cold spell most likely resulted from volcanic activity in Iceland. For several years, colder weather had been the subject of much speculation, and in 1784, even Benjamin Franklin weighed in on it.

> During several of the summer months of the year 1783, when the effect of the sun's rays to heat the earth in these northern regions should have been greater, there existed a constant fog over all Europe, and a great part of North America. This fog was of a permanent nature; it was dry, and the rays of the sun seemed to have little effect towards dissipating it, as they easily do a moist fog, arising from water. They were indeed rendered so faint in passing through it, that when collected in the focus of a burning glass they would scarce kindle brown paper. Of course, their summer effect in heating the Earth was exceedingly diminished.
>
> Hence the surface was early frozen.
>
> Hence the first snows remained on it unmelted, and received continual additions.
>
> Hence the air was more chilled, and the winds more severely cold.
>
> Hence perhaps the winter of 1783–4 was more severe than any that had happened for many years.
>
> The cause of this universal fog is not yet ascertained. Whether it was adventitious to this earth, and merely a smoke, proceeding from the consumption by fire of some of those great burning balls or globes which we happen to meet with in our rapid course round the sun, and which are sometimes seen to kindle and be destroyed in passing our atmosphere, and whose smoke might be attracted and retained by our earth; or whether it was the vast quantity of smoke, long continuing; to issue during the summer from Hecla in Iceland, and that other volcano which arose out of the sea near that island, which smoke might be spread by various winds, over the northern part of the world, is yet uncertain.
>
> It seems however worth the enquiry, whether other hard winters, recorded in history, were preceded by similar permanent and widely extended summer fogs. Because, if found to be so, men might from such fogs conjecture the probability of succeeding hard winter, and of the damage to be expected by the breaking up of frozen rivers in the spring; and take such measures as are possible and practicable, to secure themselves and effects from the mischiefs that attended the last.[2]

Franklin attributed the weather to an Icelandic volcano, but it was not Hecla that erupted at that time. In the period from 1783 to 1785, two volcanoes in Iceland, Laki and Grimsvotn, erupted, spewing out basalt lava clouds and sulfur dioxide compounds that killed more than half of Iceland's livestock. Clouds of ash travelled around the globe, affecting the weather. Also, in April of 1785, the Aogashima volcano erupted in Japan, adding to the atmospheric mix.

These volcanoes were almost certainly the cause of the colder temperatures, and were also very likely responsible for the Dark Day on November 24th. Note Franklin's description of a fog which reduced sunlight. It's possible, however, that other conditions contributed to the Dark Day. On May 19, 1780, New England experienced a Dark Day which was later discovered to have resulted from a combination of distant forest fires, cloud cover, and thick fog.

Whatever the cause, however, it was unknown by Clark and Bankston, who "spoke in whispers," and by the Indians who came to the circle at Yamacutah and gazed at the statue. Their mysterious gathering shows that in 1785, there were still Indians who had not lost contact with the meaning of Yamacutah, or who, if they had, sought to regain something which connected them to the spiritual lives of their ancestors.

The presence of Clark and Bankston marked the beginning of the end of Yamacutah as a sacred site. This beautiful place in the wilderness had been so connected with the Great Spirit, that no human in memory had ever impinged upon its sanctity by killing so much as a bird there. Where else could there have been a place so pristine, completely untouched by death? It's hard to imagine. Yet Jordan Clark and Jacob Bankston unwittingly undid perhaps centuries of peace by killing a bear.

Perhaps the cold spring and the Dark Day, caused by far away events, still spoke personally to the native peoples who felt their sacred places slipping away from them.

In 1785, the Creek Confederacy reluctantly ceded most of northeast Georgia, because so much illegal settlement had occurred that it was untenable for the Creeks. Within two generations, a myth would begin that this region had always been Cherokee. Towns would spring up, and the site would be lost. It no longer has a place in any living person's memory, but because it was saved in Clark and Bankston's account, and by Wilson, it has a life in all our imaginations. Yamacutah . . . otherworldly, quiet and beautiful.

Dark Day at Yamacutah, November 24, 1785

Virtual reality image by Richard Thornton, Architect

REFERENCES AND NOTES

1. Jones, John Colcock, **Monumental Remains of Georgia**, Savannah: John M. Cooper and Company, 1861.

2. Sparks, Jared, **The Works of Benjamin Franklin Vol.VI**, Boston: Hilliard, Gray, and Company, 1840.

3. Wilson, Gustavus J.N., **The Early History of Jackson County, Georgia, Second Edition**, Atlanta: Foote & Davies Co., 1914.

LIST OF ILLUSTRATIONS

(cont'd.)

www.ingramcontent.com/pod-product-compliance
Lightning Source LLC
Chambersburg PA
CBHW080518090426
42734CB00015B/3095